HOW TO DEVELOP CLAIRVOYANCE

Describes four varieties of clairvoyant experience,
including the ability to foretell future events. Also
gives techniques for developing latent clairvoyance
and instructions for making a sand disc and a black
mirror, both acceptable substitutes for a crystal.

G000245762

HOW TO DEVELOP CLAIRVOYANCE

By

W. E. BUTLER

THE AQUARIAN PRESS
Wellingborough, Northamptonshire

First published 1968
Sixth Impression 1977
Second Edition, revised, enlarged
and reset, 1979
Second Impression 1981
Third Impression 1984

ISBN 0 85030 169 6 (UK)
ISBN 0 87728 409 1 (USA)

Printed in Great Britain by
Richard Clay (The Chaucer Press),
Bungay, Suffolk.

CONTENTS

PREFACE

At the request of my publishers, I have added a preface and some additional material to this revised printing of my book on the development of clairvoyance.

What has become known as the 'occult explosion' – the sudden world-wide interest in esoteric matters – has resulted in arousing a determination of a great many people to undertake practical psychic development. Human nature being what it is, and not as we would like it to be, there are many who 'rush in where angels fear to tread', and since occult science is no more foolproof than any other science, mistakes, some of them serious, have been made by some of those who, with very little knowledge, have experimented in this field.

Because of this, panic warnings have been given by people who, in a great many cases, had very little knowledge of the subject, and they have spoken of 'dabbling in psychism or occultism'. Naturally, this irrational objection is resented by those who are serious workers in these fields, but it is as well to remember that dabbling in any subject – save perhaps Bingo or Dominoes – can lead to trouble. But the dabblers do not amount to more than a small section of those who are studying psychic and occult matters, and the best thing we can do for these 'amateurs of the subconscious', as they have been termed, is to show them the correct methods of development, and so help them to refrain from foolish and ignorant experiments.

However, despite the strictures of its enemies, true occultism does *not* encourage ignorant and foolish experimentation. It is, within its own limits, a true science, and as such it has its own laws and methods of research. It is within the context of these that I have written this book. However 'of the making of books there is no end' and books vary greatly in their presentation of these subjects. What then should be the criteria by which the newcomer may evaluate them? My own opinion is that they should never be approached in an uncritical spirit. A healthy scepticism is preferable to a foolish acceptance of every statement made in any book dealing with these subjects – including my own!

At the same time, there is a *pathological* scepticism which goes far beyond reasonable limits, and the reader should be prepared to change his opinions should what he reads appeal to his reason. It is not easy for anyone to change his lifelong ideas and the process can be very painful. However, there are many people who, for one reason or another, are already seeking for new insights into life, and they may be tempted to accept more than they should – at least at the beginning of their studies. As they proceed they will begin to appreciate the value of that wise Eastern saying 'Discrimination is the first virtue of the Path'. In one of the prayers of the Anglican Church, the student of the Scriptures is advised to 'read, mark, learn and *inwardly digest* them'. This holds the key to understanding and wisdom, more the words I have italicized. So many students of these matters appear to have acquired a vast amount of surface knowledge, but to have made no attempt to reduce it to a workable system, and it is these people, who tend to be blown about by every shift in the wind of current opinion, who are the worst enemies of the true occult schools. Such people have gained much knowledge, but Wisdom eludes them.

This book is intended for those who perhaps for the first time are enquiring into these matters. I would ask them to approach it as I have indicated, stick to the rules and judge by the results they obtain.

Totton,   W.E. Butler
Hampshire.

CHAPTER ONE

WHAT IS CLAIRVOYANCE?

The word clairvoyance with its associated words 'clairaudience' and 'clairsentience' comes from the French, and these were used by the followers of Dr Franz Anton Mesmer, who popularized the practice of what was then known as 'Animal Magnetism' later to be called after him by the term 'Mesmerism'. A certain amount of mesmeric work was later re-christened by Dr James Braid. He called it 'Hypnotism' and under his name that particular fragment of the mesmeric technique has become respectable; there is even a 'Medical Society of Hypnotists'! Drs Esdaile and Elliotson, together with many others of their profession who were bitterly persecuted by the medical orthodoxy of their day, must surely have smiled, a little ruefully perhaps, when in the after-life they were told of the formation of a Society of *Medical* Hypnotists.

E.S.P.

In the course of their researches, the early mesmerists discovered that some of their patients, when in the deep mesmeric trance showed signs of what today is known as E.S.P. – Extra-Sensory Perception. They didn't have this very convenient term so they used other names, such as those we have already given. However, in modern times new names have been given, many of them derived from Greek and Latin words. This is because there was, and still is, a great deal of superstition, silliness and fraud associated with the old names, and it was felt necessary to break away from the old associations. In this respect, the poet was possibly right when he asked 'What's in a name?' The flower of supernormal vision is just as real a thing when it is called 'metagnomy' or E.S.P., as when it is known as 'clairvoyance'.

The three words 'clairvoyance', 'clairaudience' and 'clairsentience' mean 'clear vision', 'clear hearing' and 'clear sensing' respectively, and, of course they do not refer to the ordinary physical senses, but rather to super-normal or superphysical sense perceptions. Since, however, these superphysical perceptions do not enter our minds through our physical senses, where, then, *do* they have their origin? The short answer, and one which we believe to be correct, is that they come from the subconscious levels of our mind. As you know, modern psychology has shown that certain levels of the mind exist behind or below the ordinary waking consciousness, and it is in these levels that clairvoyance has its point of emergence. For the purpose of this book we may be somewhat dogmatic, and to simplify the issue may say that we all possess a finer body of superphysical substance, and that the 'senses' of that finer body can be connected to the waking consciousness so that what we perceive in those finer levels of substance may be *consciously* perceived, for it is fairly certain that even though we may not consciously receive these superphysical sense reports, they are being constantly received in the deeper mind both when we are awake and when we sleep.

'Stained-Glass Effect'

In the East there has been worked out an elaborate scheme of psychic development which refers to an intricate set of links, which are known as 'the *Chakras*', which can be developed in order that superphysical perceptions may be brought *through* the subconsciousness, and this is true, of course, of the real supernormal powers. There are, however, many cases of visions, voices and other sense-perceptions where it is fairly easy for the psychologist to prove that they originate *in* the subconscious and are, in fact, due to certain stresses and strains therein. There is a great difference between the E.S.P. images and those born in the subconsciousness, but in *both cases* the images, sounds, and so on are built up in accordance with the laws governing the workings of that subconscious level. It is important that you should realize that although your visions may be genuine E.S.P., they are likely to become somewhat distorted as they pass through to your waking self. This distorting action is well known to all who have had practical experience of these matters. The late W.T. Stead, the veteran journalist and social reformer called this 'the stained glass effect', and this gives a very good picture of the action of the subconscious. Just as a stained-glass window imposes its own patterns and colours upon the white light which streams through it, so does the subconscious stain and distort all that passes through it to the waking self.

Voluntary and Involuntary Nervous System

As a matter of fact, even when we are using our ordinary physical senses the same distorting action takes place, though to a lesser degree. We see that which our subconscious 'keys' us to see, and often entirely miss things which are seen by others who are looking at the same scene. This is well known to police and lawyers, who have to deal with eye-witness accounts of accidents, and other occurrences. It is asserted by occultists that the incoming clairvoyant or other psychic impressions may make use of two different nerve systems in our body. They may come by ways of what is known as the 'involuntary nervous system' or by way of the 'cerebro-spinal system'. If they come via the involuntary nervous system, the 'Gates of Ivory' as they were known in ancient times, they may be vague and difficult to define. The images themselves may be clear, but the meanings which they are intended to deliver to the waking self are not clearly perceived. Also, in very many cases, this form of vision is not under the control of the will of the person concerned. Often when it is needed, it cannot be brought into action, and at other times when it is not required, it breaks through into the waking consciousness. You will easily see that this could be dangerous under certain circumstances. The other mode of working through the voluntary nervous system, has the advantage of being under the control of the psychic, and can be aroused at will. It is also far less dependent upon what, in psychic experimentation, are known as 'conditions'.

However, having told you all this, we must also tell you that the use of one form of psychism alone is very rare, despite what some of the 'authorities' may say. Over fifty years of practical experience in this field has taught us that it is very seldom that the so-called 'positive psychic' is entirely using the voluntary nerve system. He may achieve ninety-nine per cent of such control on good days, but on others he may be only fifty-five per cent 'positive'. In the same way the psychic using the involuntary nervous system may, on very good days, begin to work through the voluntary nerves. In fact, both 'positive' and 'negative' psychics work on a kind of sliding-scale for the two nerve systems are closely linked together. Although the voluntary system should be the dominant partner, all the processes by which the senses, whether they be physical or superphysical, communicate their messages to the waking self are processes which are carried out by the involuntary nervous system working through the machinery of the subconscious mind.

We have said this because we wish to blur the distinction which has been established by many theoretical occultists between the two forms of psychic activity. At the same time we do want to emphasize that you *must* establish some measure of control over your psychic activity right from the moment you commence your training. Of course, during the early stages of that training you have to give the developing faculty a considerable amount of leeway, but, gently and persistently, voluntary control must be imposed on it.

Extension of Physical Sight
It is quite possible, bearing in mind the current attitude to the subject, that your ideas as to what clairvoyance really is are somewhat mixed. The name is applied to so many things, and this often leads to considerable confusion. So we will try to describe in as simple a way as possible, what clairvoyance is. First of all, however, we want to

deal with a form of clairvoyance which is in reality an extension of the ordinary physical sight. If you take a prism, which is, as you know, a three-sided glass bar, and pass a beam of white light through it, the white light is split up into a band of colours ranging from red at the one end to violet at the other. We know also, that below the colour vibration red there are infra-red rays, and above or beyond the violet end of this coloured spectrum are other rays, including the ultra-violet rays, the X-rays and many others. In fact our visible band of colours is only a section of a very great range of vibration.

Now if, having thrown your coloured band of light on to a white background, you invite half a dozen people to mark just where, on the white card, the limits of the colour band seem to them to be situated, you will find that the results will vary in sometimes a spectacular way. You may find that one person places the limits well *within* the red end, and well *beyond* the violet end. Others will apparently see more beyond the red end and even see less of the violet end. Most of the people with whom you do this experiment will see the band of colour in the same general way, but you will have those who seem to see more at one end than at the other. This particular variation depends upon the structure of the retina: the screen in the eye upon which the lens of the eye projects a picture of whatever you may be looking at. There are, of course, other factors, but these are not recognized by the orthodox medical faculty, as they belong to the super-physical levels.

Now this experiment shows that some people are able to perceive light vibrations which are invisible to others, and this is why we have referred to this experiment. Through the years a very considerable amount of experimental proof has been obtained in support of the teachings of the followers of Mesmer, and others too, that the physical body has a counterpart of much finer matter, and that this finer body is the mould upon which the physical body is built up. This finer body is the mould upon which the physical body is built up. This finer body also has its senses, and these are capable of perceiving the various conditions of the world of finer matter of which this 'etheric body' is built up.

Etheric Double

The use of the name etheric arouses a good deal of contempt from the physicists, who regard the word 'ether' as one of their own particular possessions, though the latest fashion in physics does, I believe, reject any such thing as the ether of space. Fashions change even in science. However, there have been other names given to this finer physical body. In ancient Egypt it was known as the *Ka*, in medieval Germany as the *Doppelganger*, in certain Rosicrucian Schools as the 'vital body' and in Modern Theosophy as the 'etheric double'. The French spiritists refer to it as the 'peri-sprit'.

It is taught that through the etheric double the vital forces enter the physical body, and that the mind and emotions are able to be expressed through all the cells, glands and nerves of the body. It is also taught that the senses of this finer body can also be linked up with the waking consciousness, and there are certain methods of doing this. We will discuss this matter of the development of etheric vision and audition when we come to deal with the actual work of psychic training.

The etheric vision is sometimes called 'X-ray vision' as it allows its possessor to see through physical matter. In the early days of mesmerism it was developed for the medical diagnosis of diseases, and since the etheric clairvoyant can, in some cases, apparently see into the interior of the human body and closely observe the working of the various organs therein, it is easy to see how very helpful this form of clairvoyance can be.

Developing Etheric Vision

There are certain devices which, it is claimed, enable this form of vision to be developed. Special dyes, such as the coal-tar dye dycyanine, are dissolved in alcohol, and the liquid poured into a cell formed by cementing together two pieces of plain glass, leaving a small gap between them. The experimenter looks at a source of light through this coloured screen for a certain time and then, after some perseverance in the technique, he may begin to see the emanations which are constantly being given off by all living things. The theory is that the practice alters the retina or screen of the eye (the 'rods' and 'cones' as the minute nerve endings which make up that screen are called) thus enabling the eye to respond to rays of light which are beyond the visible coloured spectrum. There are also spectacles, 'auraspecs' as they are called, with coloured glass inserts, which, it is claimed, produce the same effect as the dycyanine screens.

The pioneer work on this line of research was

done by a medical electrician, W.J. Kilner at St Thomas' Hospital in London, a good many years ago. He published an account of his work in a book entitled *The Human Aura*. I hope to deal with etheric sight in another book in this series covering the aura and its phenomena.

Having dealt in a general way with this etheric clairvoyance, we will go on to other types, and here we may divide our subject into four fairly definite varieties of working. We have, therefore:

(*a*)   Psychological Clairvoyance.
(*b*)   Spatial Clairvoyance.
(*c*)   Astral Clairvoyance.
(*d*)   True Spiritual Clairvoyance.

In the next chapter, we will consider these four aspects of our subject, and then, having given you a fair foundation we will proceed to the actual work of development.

CHAPTER TWO

TYPES OF CLAIRVOYANCE

In the last chapter, we listed four varieties of clairvoyant experience. We shall deal with them separately, though in actual practice it is always difficult to do this, since the faculty which we are using along any one level, although directed by us along that level, may well suddenly bring in new levels of perception, when we are not desiring their manifestation. However, for convenience of study

we will differentiate between these forms of the
faculty and deal with them separately.

Psychological Clairvoyance

This is a name which we have invented ourselves, to
cover a certain type of clairvoyance, and we think
that when you have read what we have to say about
it, you will be able to see why we chose the name.
Most of us are familiar with those curious
attractions and repulsions which we feel for many
people. 'I do not like thee, Dr Fell' runs the old
verse, and it goes on to say 'The reason why, I
cannot tell'. There *are* some people whom we
instinctively and spontaneously like or dislike, and
very often the reason why we cannot tell, is that
feeling comes to us from the depths of our
subconsciousness. However, *it need not* necessarily
be due to clairvoyant perception; there is a perfectly
sound psychological explanation of this sympathy
or antipathy. It may be as well if we get this purely
psychological point out of the way before we go any
further.

In most of our lives there have been some people
who, in one way or another, have caused us to
experience pain or shame or fear on the one hand,
and joy, happiness and confidence on the other. We
have forgotten the people and the incidents with
which they were connected, and for many years we
may never have even thought of them at all.
However, the memories have not been lost, they
have simply been pushed down out of sight into the
depths of the subconscious. It is very important, if
we would maintain true psychological balance and
self-control, that such memories should *not* be
pushed down *too* deeply into the depths, as under

these circumstances they may become a kind of
mental and emotional cancer, blocking the free flow
of vitality and interfering with the orderly working
of the mind.

However, such memories are very often forgotten,
even though they are not pushed so far down into
the mind. Then one day we meet someone whose
face or bearing strongly resembles that of our
former friend or enemy, and although we do not
consciously remember that person, the newly met
person strikes a chord in our memory. Although the
mental recollection of the friend or enemy of old does
not arise, something else does, and that is the
emotional effect, the feelings which used to be
aroused, and this emotional charge is projected
upon the stranger we have met. So we feel that 'Dr
Fell', who may quite possibly be a good and
likeable man, is someone we must distrust and fear.
This psychological projection is quite common; we
had a personal instance of it only the other day, and
it does explain many of the sudden likings and
dislikings which affect us.

In many other cases, however, subsequent events
prove that our instinct was perfectly correct. Here
we come to a point which is often overlooked when
clairvoyance is being discussed. We are liable to
think of clairvoyance as simple vision, but it is quite
different. This psychic faculty, as it comes up
through the subconscious levels brings much more
with it than a simple visual picture; there is also a
combined mental and emotional atmosphere or
'effect' which surrounds it, and it is the sum of
visual image, emotional feeling and mental ideas
which come into the waking consciousness when we
exercise the clairvoyant faculty. We shall see this

again when we come to consider the part played by symbols in clairvoyance.

At the commencement of development, this mixed emotional-mental atmosphere is usually more vivid than any simple visual image, but, as it proceeds, the image becomes more definite, and the atmosphere less prominent. Following upon this, the visual images seem to give way to some extent to a curious, formless, intuitional understanding, and this may well become an entirely formless perception, in which all the details which the visual images and the mental-emotional atmosphere gave are superseded by a clear and exceedingly definite perception which, without picture or atmosphere gives to the waking self a full, definite and comprehensive understanding of whatever is being observed.

Three Levels of Perception

We do not say that this will be the automatic sequence of development. You may find the first stage to be the one which seems best *for you*. Others may find that they seem to start on the second level, where image and intuition work together, and others again may find themselves starting on the third level of perception. We may perhaps illustrate this point by an imaginary example of the workings of these three phases. Suppose we are called in to a so-called haunted house, and we take with us three clairvoyants, each working on a different level of perception. Let us see what our clairvoyant of the first level would probably experience. Sitting in the haunted room, he might see faint patches of phosphorescence in various parts, faintly luminous clouds wreathing around him, and he would 'feel' very strongly certain emotional currents in the room. These would cause similar emotions to arise in his mind, emotions of depression and gloom. As the power intensified, he might possibly see the faintly luminous figure of an elderly man sitting in the chair opposite, staring moodily at the fireplace. (This description is based upon an actual experience which we had some years ago, when we were called upon to exorcize the ghost who haunted this room.) With our clairvoyant of the first type, the atmosphere would be far more definite than the image of the man, and he would be liable to react to this atmosphere in a marked way.

Our clairvoyant of the second type would not be affected so strongly by the atmosphere of depression and gloom, but he would be able to observe the visual image of the man more closely and calmly, and he would quite possibly become aware that what he was looking at was not the real man, but an imprint or shade of someone who had lived in that house and used that room. There is a subtle but real difference between these imprints on the psychic atmosphere and the presence of a living being. It is difficult to describe the difference; gradually one becomes aware of the quality of the life within the form which is perceived. In this case our clairvoyant would find a curious unreal feeling with this form, whereas if he were looking at a living being, he would feel the personal power and individuality of the man. We shall return to this point when we consider the question of symbols and their use in clairvoyance.

Our third type of clairvoyant would, as it were, 'run up the scale'. Opening up his clairvoyant faculty, he would first become aware of the strongly charged psychic atmosphere of the room, and then, stepping up his perception, he would see, clearly and distinctly, the form which his two friends had also seen. Like the second seer, he would know that the form was simply 'an image in the astral light', as he might describe it. Now, stepping up his vision, he would for a moment or two lose both form and atmosphere, and into his mind would rise a 'block of knowledge', if we may so describe it. He would know, without a shadow of doubt, how the atmosphere of gloom, depression and suicide had been built in that room; he would know also how it had been maintained in such power since its first creation, and he would be aware of what steps must be taken to destroy it and cleanse the place that it might once again be habitable.

Atmospheres

In this particular case, the clairvoyant diagnosis and later treatment which we were able to give proved effective, and on making enquiries, we found that our clairvoyant findings were correct. We found that some ten years before our visit, the tenant at that time was a rather dull-witted farm labourer. For many years before his death by suicide he had been in the habit of returning from his work, sitting in this room and brooding over his real and imaginary wrongs. Finally he had committed suicide. The atmosphere he had left behind him was pretty deadly, as we can vouch from our own experience; we felt the strong suicidal impulse ourselves, and it was a common experience of anyone who sat in that room for any length of time.

This was an actual experience, but if you wish to

read a fictional representation by a master of the
storyteller's art, we can recommend you to read one
of Rudyard Kipling's short stores entitled 'The
House Surgeon'. There is a poem which goes with
it, called 'The Rabbi's Song', and one verse of this
may be of interest to you:

> If thought can reach to Heaven, on Heaven let it
> dwell,
> For fear like power is given to thought, to reach to
> Hell;
> For fear the desolation and darkness of thy mind
> Perplex and vex a dwelling which thou has left
> behind.

Of course, there are powerful and beneficient
forces and influences which radiate from the very
stones of those places which, through the centuries,
have been true houses of prayer and praise, and
where the two worlds have drawn closely together
through the work of faithful pastors and loving
people. These atmospheres may be perceived by the
clairvoyant, and you will learn by direct experience
that you, too, have a grave responsibility for those
conditions which you are continually forming
around you for the help or hindrance of your fellow
man. For it is indeed true, as the Bible says: 'No
man liveth to himself alone'.

We trust that this illustration of clairvoyant
practice will enable you to see what we have been
driving at in these last few pages. Clairvoyance is
not quite so simple as some would make it out to be,
but these three levels are those generally
encountered. Clairvoyance along these lines is also
of great assistance in what we may term 'psychic

counselling' and clairvoyants of all three types can do good work therein. If we have made it appear that the third type is the best of the three, it is not because we wish you to regard the other two as being inferior. They *are* inferior in one sense, since they are stages in the development of the third type, and this we regard as the highest aspect of *this* level of psychic perception. There are higher levels, but these we shall deal with when we come to the form of clairvoyance which we have termed Spiritual Clairvoyance.

Clairvoyance in Space and Time

We now come to what we have named Spatial Clairvoyance: that is, clairvoyance in space and time. Here we find two different methods used by clairvoyants of this kind. To explain this, we must go back to the time of the American Civil War. A certain General Polk found that whenever he touched a piece of brass, even in pitch-darkness, he experienced a curious metallic taste. This isolated fact interested a Dr Rhodes Buchanan, who experimented with his students by getting them to hold phials containing powerful drugs. He found that some of the students, almost immediately after holding such phials, began to show the symptoms which would have been produced in them by an actual dose of the drug in question. His researches, in turn, attracted the attention of Professor Denton, a noted geologist of his time, who experimented with the aid of his sister, Mrs Ann Denton Cridge.

He found that if she held a geological specimen to her forehead, she was able to see, in visual images, something of its past history. He carried out an exhaustive series of tests, in which he cut out any possibility of telepathic action between himself and his sister. The results of his researches were published in a book entitled *The Soul of Things*. This power of reading the past through the use of some object as a centre of concentration he named 'psychometry', a word which is made up from two Greek words which mean 'the soul' and 'a measure'. So psychometry, to Denton, was the gift which enabled a person to measure the soul of things; to gain from an object the story of its history. Since Denton's time, modern psychologists have used the word psychometry in a totally different way, and, curiously enough, they grumble about the spiritualists and their allies using the word in the sense in which it was originally understood. A good dictionary will give you both meanings of the word.

In its simplest terms, psychometry is really clairvoyance in time, using an object as a starting point and point of reference. Actually, it can be exercised without using an object, but concentration upon it helps to keep the clairvoyant faculty working within certain chosen limits. As we say, the object can be omitted and many people exercise this clairvoyance in time without having any idea of what they are doing. Some find that, although they are not aware of possessing any psychic power, when they are touching old furniture or antiques, dim pictures and emotions arise in their minds. This dim clairvoyant perception is far more common than is generally realized.

'Anima Mundi'

It is fairly easy for us to think of a cosmic picture-gallery; a kind of living cinematographic record of everything that has happened in the world. It has been called the *Anima Mundi*: the 'Soul of the World', and in the East, the Akashic Record. In ancient Egypt the record which was read out when the soul of a dead person was judged in the after-life was understood to be this imperishable record, and in the Christian Bible, in the Revelation of St John, it is said that the books were opened, and the souls were judged by their record. It is possible that this image of the Book of Records was in the mind of the seer who wrote the Book of Revelation, but it may also be that in both religions there was a knowledge of the existence of this cosmic record.

Now we come to a very different and difficult aspect of the subject. We can understand the record of all that *has* happened being preserved in such a way as we have described, but how about those things which have not yet happened, but which are sometimes perceived by the clairvoyant? That such prevision is possible is established beyond any doubt. This aspect of clairvoyance in time is one which has been the greatest attraction which this subject could offer, and through all recorded history this power of prevision has been sought after in all cultures and by many means. Some of these ways of bringing the faculty into action have been good, others have been most decidedly evil. For the developing clairvoyant this power of prevision is a very great attraction and a very great danger. It seems so wonderful to be able to foretell the future, that the young psychic is swept off his feet by a feeling of importance as he is consulted by those who desire to know something of that which is going to happen to them in the future. Herein lies the danger, and it is a two-fold one. First of all, the feeling of importance may grow to such an extent as to make him an egomaniac, and secondly, he will tend to overwork his faculty and then find that it is no longer reliable.

Prevision and Probability

How the faculty works we do not yet really understand, though there are many theories, some of which cover some parts of the facts and others which cover other parts. However, there is one form of prevision which can bear a rational explanation. If we think of a man who is standing at the window of a tall block of flats, looking down upon a busy street, we may picture him watching the progress of a lady who is doing a little window-shopping on the opposite side of the road. As his eyes range along the street he may also see a painter on top of a tall ladder and, just before the lady reaches the foot of that ladder, he may see the painter drop his paint-can, which begins to fall towards the pavement. Estimating the speed at which the paint is falling, and the speed at which the lady is approaching the spot where the paint-can will hit the pavement, our observer would be fully justified if he called out to the lady 'You are going to have an accident in a moment!' *If* she continues at her present speed, and does not turn to look at some window display which catches her eye, and *if* the pot of paint continues to fall without hitting any projection on the building, the prophecy of our observer may well come true. But if the other factors we have mentioned *do* come into the picture, then the prophecy will fail or, if the paint splashes over a considerable area, the lady may have her dress spotted with paint from the burst tin, and therefore may be said to have had a slight accident.

This is a possible explanation of some prevision, though not of all. The clairvoyant observer sees the possible working out of certain forces connected with the person concerned, and as long as those forces continue as they are, then the result may be calculated in the deeper mind of the clairvoyant. In other cases, however, this explanation is not possible, and we are driven to attempt to understand the paradox that a future *effect* may come before its *cause*. This, of course, seems to violate all the laws of mind, but in the realms of physics there are one or two significant things which seem to point to this possibility; for instance the observed fact that an electron, under certain conditions, can apparently be at two places at once!

This whole subject is bound up with the philosophic ideas of Fate and Free Will, of the sequence of Action and Reaction, and is the happy hunting ground of all kinds of theorists, cranks and pseudo-philosophers. Fourth Dimensions, Fifth Dimension and many other terms are used with an air of knowledge, but we can well ignore them. Let us be pragmatic, and simply say, 'Prevision is a fact. How it works we do not know, at present!'

In any case, it will be the practice of foretelling the future, rather than the theories about it, which will concern you when you have begun to develop your clairvoyant powers and have been unwise enough to tell your friends about it. Those who don't regard you as a case for psychiatric treatment may cause you a lot of trouble by their naive belief in the accuracy of your clairvoyance. To the general public the word clairvoyance means one or both of two things: you can either see spirits or you can foretell the future; or do both of these things. However, the discerning of spirits is not so easy as the uninstructed seem to think, and the foretelling of the future has its own pitfalls. There are very few clairvoyants who can steadily and consistently exercise the power of prevision, for you must bear in mind that the very fact that you are clairvoyant does not guarantee you prevision. All depends upon the kind of clairvoyant faculty you may develop.

Telling Fortunes

However, you will be besieged by those who want their fortunes told and, if your clairvoyance does give you prevision, you must then decide whether it is right *for you* to employ it for this purpose. This is not an easy matter; so much depends upon the conditions of your life. As a general rule, however, such a use of the power should be very sparingly exercised.

There are certain devices, such as the use of tea-leaves or coffee grounds left in a cup, which can be used by the clairvoyant to direct his vision to the future and, of course, there are the Tarot Cards. Sand Geomancy and the I'Ching which may be used to awaken the clairvoyant faculty and direct it along this line of prevision. The power of all these methods lies in the operator himself, *not* in the tea-leaves, coffee grounds, Tarot pictures, Geomantic dots in the sand or the positions taken up by the falling sticks of the I'Ching.

There is a very real test which you must face. In this foretelling of the future, you are entering into a close relationship with the inner lives of those who consult you, with their hopes and fears and doubts.

Your slightest word will be taken by many of these people to be the voice of truth, and they will try to order their lives by your foretelling. Have you the moral right to put yourself in the position of the oracle? Your findings will be powerful suggestions acting on the minds of your sitters. Will you be able to bear the responsibility which you have accepted? Should one of your clients misunderstand your message, and thinking it means that disaster awaits her, commit suicide, will you be able to justify yourself at the bar of your conscience? These and many other issues are bound up in this question of fortune-telling, and you will need to think the matter over very seriously before coming to any decision.

Indeed, in all clairvoyant work you will begin to realize that you must be most careful in what you describe, and especially in the inferences which you draw from what you see.

Astral Clairvoyance

Now we come to the next type of clairvoyance, which we have called Astral Clairvoyance. By this we mean the perception of apparently living beings who have no physical body.

The *Devas* or 'Shining Ones', the 'Lordly Ones' of Celtic tradition, the naiads, the dryads and the oreads of Grecian belief, and the fairy-folk, the Spirits of the Elements; all these live and have their being in the etheric and astral realms. Some of these entities you may see as your clairvoyance begins to unfold, and their activities form a fascinating field of study for the clairvoyant investigator.

It is in this field of clairvoyant work that you will need to exercise the greatest care, for you will be making conscious contact with living beings of many different kinds, and not all of them will be friendly. You will also have to cultivate the power to resist the glamour which some of these beings can exert over you unless you have so trained yourself to resist this.

The matter of that realm of existence which we have termed the astral levels is very different from that of the physical world, and this can cause you considerable confusion in your first clairvoyant adventures in these realms. Here on earth, matter is stable and if we wish to build something; a house, for example, we have to move various bits of matter from one place to another: bricks, tiles, beams, cement, and so on. Whether we employ mechanical help, or use our own physical energy, we are always working against what we may call the weight and inertia of physical matter.

On the astral levels, however, things are very different for the substance of that world is not so dense and inert, but plastic and capable of being moulded by the power of thought and desire. So the astral scenery which you will begin to see if your clairvoyance develops along this line is built up by the thoughts and emotions of those who dwell therein.

There are beings existing only on these astral and etheric levels and they create their own scenery and conditions, though these are of a kind which are unintelligible to the human mind until it has been trained to perceive such non-human effects.

Because of the plastic nature of the astral, it is difficult for the clairvoyant who is just beginning to open up his psychic vision to find his way around; he is bewildered by the complexity of the world into

which he is gazing. Because of this, and because of
his own earth-conditioned consciousness, he will
without a doubt make many mistakes before he can
correctly understand that which he perceives in
psychic vision.

Non-Human Intelligences

The non-human intelligences of this astral level
do not possess any form similar to that of man, but
they *do* have their own forms, though these cannot
be described in earth terms. If the human
clairvoyant does come into contact with such non-
human beings, his subconsciousness gives to them
'a local habitation and a name'. This usually is
embodied in a traditional image. Thus, the
elemental lives of the four modes of matter, the four
elements, so-called, were visualized in medieval
times as Gnomes, Sylphs, Undines and
Salamanders. In other nations and at other times,
they were given different forms by man, and
Shakespeare in *A Midsummer Night's Dream* has
caused innumerable 'fairy-forms' to be built up by
the visualizing imaginations of countless theatre
goers. Such forms are quickly seized and made use
of by the elemental spirits, and in such guises they
are often seen by clairvoyants.

So in many ways, this great world of the astral is
well-named the World of Illusion. At the same time,
the illusions are in the *artificially created appearances* of
that world; in itself it is as real as any other realm of
Nature. We have given you this very brief outline of
the astral conditions so that you may realize
something of the amazing complexity of the subject,
but for the purpose for which this book has been
written, it is not necessary to go further into any

detailed consideration of the astral levels. Unless you undertake very special psychic investigation such detail is not really necessary – though, of course, the more you *do* know, the better are you able to use your gift. But just as, in earthly life, you gradually developed your powers and learnt by experience to use them, so in this psychic realm, experience is quite a good teacher.

Spiritual Clairvoyance

We come now to the last type of clairvoyance – that which we have termed Spiritual Clairvoyance. Before we start to deal with this type of vision, we will consider the word 'spiritual', as it is very often entirely misunderstood. There are certain schools of thought which, so we believe, have built a very unsound body of teachings upon such misunderstandings. We say we believe this to be so, but in these matters we can only put forward what we believe to be the truth, and since the approaches to truth vary enormously, we can only speak for ourselves, or for our particular school of thought.

We want you to consider, with an open mind, the ideas we are now going to put before you. The general idea of spirit, where the idea of its reality is accepted, is of a state of being totally opposed to, and distinct from matter, more especially the matter of the material world, and of the material body we use in that world. Now this idea of the total and complete opposition of spirit and matter is a teaching which crept into Christianity in its early days, and in one form or another, it is still with us. At one time it was active in the early Church as what is known as the Manichean heresy, its originator in that particular form being a certain teacher Manes by name, who finally met his death at the hands of the Magian priests of the Persian religion of Zoroastrianism. Later in the history of the West, it reappeared as the Puritan outlook which soured the religious field of the sixteenth and seventeenth centuries. Now if matter is so absolutely evil and eternally opposed to spirit, then the best thing the religious person can do is to turn his back upon it, and concentrate entirely upon the virtues of the spirit. More particularly he should repudiate and force down all the natural instincts of the physical body he is wearing, this 'vile' body, as he would regard it.

However, there have always been those, inside Christianity as well as outside it, who have repudiated this narrow and perverted view of life. Sometimes their repudiation was overdone, and the extremely lax ideas they put forward were as bad as the over-strict ideas which they replaced. In our own day we see just such a repudiation of the Puritan outlook, and again, some are carrying their revolt to such extreme lengths that they bid fair to produce conditions which are just as bad as those which they have repudiated!

Now in the system of thought to which we give our allegiance, virtue, sanity and true spirituality lies in the point midway between the extremes. All *material things* are, we believe, just as good, just as holy as are *spiritual things*. There is no eternal enmity between spirit and matter; they are the two poles of manifest existence, and it is in the *balanced use* of both spiritual and material principles that the way of progress lies. True spirituality, then, does not mean that you repudiate the material world and all its affairs, that you repress and trample upon your material body with all its wonderful instincts and mechanisms, or that you concentrate entirely upon your own fancied 'spiritual development', ignoring all your manifest duties to your fellow men. You cannot, of course, isolate yourself entirely, for 'no man is an island', but you may so limit yourself by such an attitude that you cut down to a mere trickle the life-giving energies of the universe; energies which are essential for your healthy existence.

You may ask, what has all this to do with the development of clairvoyance? Of course, you may develop clairvoyant faculty without any religious or moral outlook in your mind; psychic faculties have nothing to do with moral or ethical rules. In fact, many of us, from long study of the subject, believe that some of the more pitiful offenders against the existing moral and ethical codes are as they are because, unknown to themselves, they are in some degree natural psychics, and are therefore open to telepathic pressures and temptations which the non-psychic does not usually experience. Therefore, without any religious or ethical standards, you may develop these psychic abilities, since they are in themselves natural powers just as are the physical senses.

Clairvoyance: A Natural Power

Everyone possesses these faculties, but how near they are to emerging from the subconscious is another matter. With some people they are near the surface; with others they are so deep that the time which would be needed to bring them into the waking consciousness could well be applied to more effective fields of endeavour. Here an analogy may help. Let us take the case of two people, one of whom appears to have been born with a strong musical sense, the other having apparently no musical ability of any kind. In the first case, a comparatively short course of music lessons would show him to be a splendid musician, but the other man would probably be just as non-musical after twenty years of lessons, and the time he has wasted in this vain effort could have been employed to better purposes. So is it with the clairvoyant faculty. It is a *natural* power. If we seem to have over-emphasized this, it is because there is a mistaken idea abroad that these faculties are 'gifts from the Gods', and we keep this mistake alive when we talk about psychic gifts. A faulty translation of part of a letter from St Paul to his Corinthian converts refers to 'spiritual gifts', but a better translation would be 'psychic gifts', and St Paul appears to be referring to the *manifestation* of these powers under the influence of the Holy Spirit. Christian theologians usually refer to them as the *charismata* or 'gifts', thus encouraging this idea of the nature of the psychic faculties. Of course, we often use words fairly loosely, as for instance when we say that such and such a person is a gifted musician or artist, or that someone is exceptionally gifted in the political or professional spheres. Here we are thinking in the thought-patterns of the classic Greeks and Romans; the gods were the givers of gifts to men, and often their reasons for so doing seemed arbitrary and illogical. Try to get clear of this old pattern of thought, and you will then be able to form a more correct idea of these things.

Of course, in the end all life, all consciousness, all faculties, come from the Divine, but all work is manifest under immutable natural law. There is but one aspect of the universe which is supernatural and that is, to use an old phrase, the Holy One 'Whom Nature hath not formed, from Whom all Nature proceeds and is governed'. So our psychic faculties are natural powers. If we get this idea firmly fixed in our minds, which is why we have repeated it so many times, and if we choose our words so that we break away from the old forms of expression, then we will be less likely to get a wrong idea of ourselves. We have not been singled out by divine power to receive something unique, but are simply in the position of having become aware of another level of perception. It has nothing to do with our personal character, neither is it in any way a substitute for religion. So we should not be unduly boastful because we have the faculty in working order, neither should we fall into the error of believing that the possession of it shows our high spiritual development. It should be pointed out, however, that the *range* of our psychic powers *does* depend upon our moral development; we can only receive that which we can tune in to, to use a radio analogy.

CHAPTER THREE

TRAINING TECHNIQUES

As in any science, art or craft, there are certain ways of proceeding, certain techniques which must be followed if we would succeed in our efforts to develop clairvoyance. Now the great trouble with the whole subject of psychic training in the past has

been its involvement with various religious and
cultural ideas. We do not mean to suggest that all
these conditions and involvements were without
their uses; indeed many of them have been of great
assistance. However, there are certain essentials
and these are what we want to deal with in this
chapter. If you find that it helps you to cultivate
your powers within the framework of some religion
or philosophy, well and good. But do not acquire
the habit into which many fall, and look with
disdain or disapproval on those who find it possible
to do without any such religious or philosophical
assistance. There is a saying 'To every man his own
master, and who art thou to judge another's
servant? To his own master he stands or falls'.

The clairvoyant faculty is an entirely natural
power, and has nothing to do with moral, ethical or
religious teaching, any more than our ordinary
eyesight depends upon whether we belong to the
Catholic Church or to the Hindu religion. It
follows, then, that the singing of hymns and the use
of various forms of prayer are not, in themselves
necessary. At the same time, if such practices are
real to us, if they have a definite meaning to us, then
they can be of the greatest value. Indeed, in the
deeper levels of development, prayer assumes a
power and reality of which we were not hitherto
aware, and we then realize what a tremendous help
it can be.

Folk-Lore and Magic

At the start of our development, we are
dependent upon aids of all kinds, but as we progress
we find that we can do without many of them. A
little careful study of the lore which has come down

to us concerning the development of the psychic faculties, soon shows that much of it comes from the curious magico-religious traditions of the Middle Ages, much is derived from a very ancient folk-lore, and a certain amount from the continued experiments of many would-be servers, as the clairvoyants are sometimes called. We can safely forget the magico-religious tradition, since it is not essential to the development of clairvoyance. Not that we decry Magic; we could hardly do that, since we have written several books on the subject, and do ourselves belong to a magical fraternity.

We can also dispense with a good deal of the folk-lore regarding clairvoyance. Some of this is based on old wives' tales, and has no basis in fact. The old wives *did* preserve and hand down some very important instructions, and these we can adapt and use today. Unfortunately, they handed down a good deal of foolishness and superstitious practice as well, and some of this is still with us. Now we come to the accounts which have been given us by those who have personally undertaken the task of clairvoyant development, and here again, their statements are coloured by their individual temperaments, and we have tried to include in this book only those parts of such statements as we consider to be of the essence of the matter.

Some of you may feel that we have left out a very important source of information on this subject, viz. the instructions in books which claim to have been written by various oriental Swamis, Gurus and Rishis. We have done this deliberately. Having a fair working knowledge of some of these Eastern systems and, indeed, some practical personal experience of their methods and the results

produced thereby, we are firmly convinced that
those exercises and teachings which are to be found
in many of these books can be both misleading and
harmful. For their safe and effective use, such
methods depend upon the *personal supervision* of a
guru or teacher who knows what he is doing, and
can observe the results of these exercises in his *chela*,
or pupil. When this can be done, then the Eastern
methods can be safely tried, although even under
these conditions it may be found that the very
different psychological outlooks of East and West
introduce some difficulties and complications.

Three Types of Consciousness

Having cleared some of the ground, we will
repeat what we have already said about the basis of
development. We think, then, of our consciousness
as being divided, like Gaul in the times of Julius
Caesar, into three parts. These are the waking
consciousness, the subconscious and the
superconscious. We may also consider the
subconscious under two aspects: the *personal aspect*
of the subconscious, and a far deeper and more
extensive level which we share with all sentient life
on this globe. This deeper level is the Collective
Unconscious described by the great psychologist Dr
C.G. Jung and his followers. First of all, if we
consider these two aspects of the mind then psychic
development consists in building up certain links
between the normal waking consciousness and the
personal subconsciousness. Owing to the conditions
under which human consciousness has evolved,
there is a barrier or division between these two
aspects of the mind, and the links which psychic
development forms have to pass through this

barrier, in order that the results of the inner clairvoyant perception may be able to rise up into the waking consciousness.

These results come through in various ways, though it is probable, indeed tradition has always maintained this, that there is but *one* psychic sense of perception. But just as all our five physical senses are modifications of the basic physical sense of touch, so the psychic faculties of clairvoyance, clairaudience and clairsentience are modifications and expressions of the one basic psychic perception.

So your success in developing clairvoyance depends upon your bringing through the psychic perceptions in a visual form. If you were trying to develop clairaudience, then you would be trying to bring through this perception in subjective sounds and words. Much of the hard work of development as a clairvoyant is cut out if you have the natural power of *visualization*, or if you have trained yourself to visualize, to build up clear images in your mind. Some people have this power of mental visualization in an extraordinary degree. We remember meeting, many years ago, a girl of between five and six years of age who had an uncanny power to draw clear outline pictures of various kinds. When we asked her how she did it, she said, 'I think, and then I draw a line round my think!' Rosalind Heywood, in her book *The Infinite Hive*, mentions this same power as used by her son in his schoolwork. This power to project a mental image so strongly as to see it apparently outside one's head is possessed by many artists, and, unfortunately, a certain type of mentally disturbed person often finds it happening involuntarily. Because such involuntary visions and voices are common symptoms of such mental trouble, all the more serious schools of thought on this subject insist upon their pupils never allowing this involuntary projection to take place. Incidentally, repeated investigations have shown that in *some* cases which have been diagnosed as purely mental illness, there was a true psychic element, and some of what certain of these people saw in visions was really due to clairvoyant perception. Perhaps the more enlightened members of the Jungian school of psychology may yet study this interesting side issue.

The psychologist Freud, writing to Dr Ernest Jones said that if he had his time over again he would study psychic research, and Carl Jung *did* take a very active interest in it.

Conscious Visualization

Should you find that your ordinary way of thinking is not along visual lines, then you will have to train yourself in conscious visualization. Here we may give you a hint which will save you a great deal of unnecessary trouble. Many of the books on the subject of visualization recommend the beginner to take a geometric form, such as a circle, a square or a triangle, and attempt to built it up in 'the mind's eye'. This can be done, but it is much easier, and just as effective, to use a picture containing numerous different details, for the mind can then move from point to point in the picture, gaining visualizing power and at the same time not becoming bored. It is this mental boredom which is possibly behind the gradual deterioration of the guesses made by Dr Rhine's subjects with the Zener Cards which he uses. It has been noticed that a subject who has been accurately predicting the cards will gradually begin to lose the ability, and it is possibly this boredom which is responsible.

Incidentally, you may find that you remember a scene or object by means of what appears to be a mental running commentary upon it. Instead of seeing in your mind's eye a patch of colour, you will simply have the *word* describing the colour appearing in your mind. If this is the case, don't worry about it, but carry on attempting to improve your *visual* power. One of the beauties of this training in visualization is that you can do it at any convenient time, and you will find that such practice greatly increases your awareness of your surroundings; a power which can be of great value in ordinary life.

We will suppose that you are naturally or by training a good visual percipient, and can build up clear visual images. You can either keep these pictures inside your head or outlined against the dark screen of the closed eyes, or you may project them outwardly and see them apparently on the surface of a crystal, mirror or other such device. Much stress is laid by some authorities upon the use of a crystal or showstone. It must be of rock crystal, though one made of glass is allowable. (Actually, crystals made of transparent plastic are on sale!) It must be magnetized by the user, employing a certain magical ceremony; it must be wrapped in silk and kept away from strong light, and sometimes the advice is that the crystal be set in a surround of ebony on which have been painted in gold the twelve Signs of the Zodiac. Others teach that it should be dedicated to a particular spirit. All this advice, in the form in which it is usually given,

can be very misleading. There is, however, a
definite reason for these instructions. Let us try to
rewrite the above list in another way. When we pick
up and examine this crystal which we have bought,
the examination of it links it in our minds with
ourselves and with the purpose for which we
purchased it. If we have a definite intention to use it
for certain types of clairvoyant work, then we have
dedicated it to a particular spirit (for the spirits
were said to rule over particular phases of the work;
the spirits of Mars, for instance, ruled over martial
happenings, the spirits of Mercury over intellectual
things). In order to prevent psychic and mental
confusion through the thoughts and emotions of
others who might see the crystal in our possession,
we keep it covered up and out of sight.

We are not saying that there are no other psychic
reasons for all these instructions. They are part of a
much greater setting in which crystals and
showstones and mirrors played, and still play, their
part, but for our present purposes they are not
necessary. Those who, like ourselves, are born
ritualists, and who find in ceremonial work a great
aid to concentration may, if we wish, do all that is
recommended in these instructions, but those to
whom such methods are distasteful may adopt the
purely mental approach we have indicated.

So far we have been referring to the crystal. But
supposing you cannot afford to buy a crystal, and a
really good crystal can be pretty expensive and even
the acrylic plastic ones are not cheap, what can you
use? You need not be worried, for there are
substitutes which can be just as effective, or even
better than the crystal. Some of these are:

1. The sand disc.
2. A sheet of white card with a large black disc painted in matt black paint in its centre.
3. A black mirror.
4. A black bowl, shallow and half-filled with ink or other dark fluid.

Making a Sand Disc

To make a sand disc, take a sheet of stout white card say 7 in. x 7 in. square, and with a pair of compasses draw a circle of 5 in. diameter in its centre. Carefully coat the inside of the circle with *ocergum* (not the modern resin glue), and while the gum is still moist, sprinkle fine sand on it. It need not necessarily be sand, any crystalline coloured powder may be used. When dry, brush off any powder which has not adhered. This sounds very easy, but a certain knack is needed, and you may find that you need to make several attempts before you have made a disc to your satisfaction. The sand disc has one rather helpful property: it does away with the vague reflections which are usually given by the crystal and mirror. These reflections of surrounding objects can be very distracting to many people, though to others they become focusing points around which the visions form.

The black disc on a white ground can be made very simply by drawing a circle on a large sheet of white card, as described in the instructions for the manufacture of the sand disc. The circle is then painted black. One of the felt-tip pencils now easily obtained from the stationers or multiple stores can be used.

Black Mirrors

The black mirror is fairly easily made. We have one which is very effective, and which was manufactured in the following way:

From a watchmaker or clockmaker obtain a circular clock-glass. This is a convex glass cover used on clock-faces. Its diameter should be about $3\frac{1}{2}$ in. though, of course, you may have it any diameter you like, within reason.

Now paint one side, the *convex* side, with black paint or enamel. You will find it best to give it two coats, allowing the first coat to thoroughly dry before applying the second. The next thing is to get something on which to mount the mirror. If you are good at wood-turning, or have a friend who is, it is possible to make a shallow bowl into which your mirror may be set leaving a frame of about one inch width around it. This frame you can stain or paint as you prefer, but we would advise you to use a subdued colour, *not* a brilliant red or yellow! You may, if you like it, paint it with gold paint. It is even quite effective to mount the mirror in an old furniture polish tin; our own is so mounted in a tin which measures just over $3\frac{1}{2}$ in. inside diameter. We supported the glass on a plaster of Paris ring. Incidentally, we once, many years ago, paid out very good and hard earned money for a black mirror, and it came duly mounted in a metal case inscribed with the signs of the Zodiac in gold. However, the mirror fell out of its case one day, and we found that the interior was also inscribed: 'Cherry Blossom Boot Polish'! We have given this instance as it adds to what we have already told you, that the crystal, the mirror, the disc, have no intrinsic power in themselves, at least as far as we are here concerned. They are simply 'autoscopes', methods by which the psychic perceptions may be brought through the subconscious levels of the mind up into the waking consciousness. We have not troubled to describe the last method, the bowl of dark fluid. The ink pool is a method used in the Middle East. It is quite effective, though again you may get distracting reflections from its surface and, things being what they are, there is an occupational risk: spilt ink!

As a footnote, we may say that one of the most brilliant clairvoyants we ever met developed his clairvoyance by using a circular black-japanned tea-tray, hung up on a wire. Judging by the results, it certainly worked well.

Mental Preparations

There are certain conditions which have to be taken into account when you decide to sit for clairvoyant development. The first of these is the state of mind in which you begin your work. It is not necessary that you should be a believer in all the myth and legend which has grown up around the subject. It is quite permissible for you to feel sceptical about the whole thing, but it is not helpful if you approach the subject in the spirit of the dying atheist who is reported to have prayed thus: 'Oh God – if there is a God – save my soul – if I have a soul!' In Scottish law there can be a verdict of Guilty, or Not Guilty or Non-proven. If you enter upon your clairvoyant development prepared to accept whatever comes, and then to work it out in the way indicated, then much which at the beginning you will feel must be placed under the heading of 'non-proven' may later be found to be suitable for either the 'true' or 'false' compartments of your thinking. So we would advise you to enter upon this path of personal psychic knowledge with an open mind, not tied to any particular dogma, but just willing to await whatever results may be obtained. This attitude is very important, since it is under these conditions that your subconscious mind is most likely to allow the psychic impressions to come into your waking mind.

Keeping Records

So much for your preliminary attitude of mind. The next important point is the question of *records*. If you are going to do serious work in this field, it is essential that from the earliest sittings you keep a detailed record of everything that happens at each sitting. It may be, in fact most probably will be, that for many sessions you will get little or nothing, but this should not prevent you from keeping records. Whatever clairvoyant visions may or may not present themselves, there are other details which should be logged. They will probably help you to find out why, at certain times, you get strong clairvoyant impressions and at other times the heavens are as brass and you get nothing at all.

Those of us who have used the clairvoyant faculty for a long time, have found that there is a curious correlation between the phases of the moon and the activity of the psychic faculties. During the waxing phase of the moon, they appear to operate more easily under the control of the will. During the waning phase, although they may appear, they are often in chaotic and unfinished forms, and no longer appear to be under the full control of the will. For this reason, the experienced clairvoyant

tends to look with a somewhat suspicious eye upon
the psychic impressions received during this period.
There are ways by which he can judge them, but
these are peculiar to each person, and are the
results of a fairly lengthy period of trial and error.
Gradually you learn to evaluate the impressions
you receive but, as we will try to describe to you
shortly, there is also a very real, though subtle
difference between the visions which come, as the
ancients said through the Gates of Horn, and those
which emerged through the Gates of Ivory.

Physical Conditions

It is probably unnecessary for us to tell you that
you are not likely to obtain good results if you have
had a violent quarrel with someone just before the
sitting, but you will find also that there are
recurrent moods which seize upon you, and which
can help or hinder your development. It is wise,
therefore, for you to enter in your record the moods
which affected you just before, during and after the
sitting. You will probably find that it all ties up
with the moon's phases, after you have gone some
months on the path of development, and can look
back over the record of that period. It is also helpful
if you make a note of the prevailing weather
conditions, as these are important. All the foregoing
points have an effect upon your mind and emotions,
but now we come to those which affect your
physical body. These are most important, for the
sensations of the physical are so strong that they
can, at the start of development, obliterate the faint
impressions coming in through the subconscious
and apart from this, the 'tone' of the physical body
has a strong effect upon the mind and emotions.

The first and most important point is that you must be *physically comfortable*. Tight clothing, tight shoes, a very hard chair, the position of the crystal or other device which causes muscular strain, all of these must be right if you are to have complete bodily relaxation. The room should be comfortably warm, but not stuffy. The temperature which should be maintained varies with each individual, but normally should not be below 60° F. This is, of course, a matter for individual preference.

Only a light meal should have been taken before the sitting; gazing at a crystal immediately after a substantial dinner will induce sleep, not psychic impressions! After the session, a light meal will be very helpful, as it tends to close down the psychic activities and restore you to normal consciousness.

Establishing a Sanctuary
Where you will sit for development depends upon the room available, and it may well be that you are not able to set aside a special room for this purpose. However, this need not be a serious obstacle, so long as it is possible for you to sit quietly and without any disturbance for the period of your session. Some people make for themselves an elaborate sanctuary into which they can retreat, and where they can employ whatever aids they feel necessary, but this is a counsel of perfection. In such a sanctuary, it is possible to use such aids as pictures which have some symbolic significance and, incense which also has its value. The latter has both a symbolic and psychological value, for by the mental law of association of ideas, the incense suggests a different atmosphere to that of everyday life. If it is used only during the sittings, then it

becomes associated in the mind with this activity, and when you enter your sanctuary and light the incense, then the mind begins automatically to concentrate itself upon the object of the sitting. However, if a separate sanctuary is not procurable, we would suggest that you do not use incense; it is not essential. One thing must be remembered in connection with this whole subject of development: all the aids which you may rightly use at the start of your training must eventually be dispensed with, so that when the faculty is fully developed, you must be able to use it under all normal conditions. The clairvoyant who is dependent upon a certain special set of circumstances before he can exercise his gift, has limited himself by this dependency upon outside things.

The lighting should be dim. Some use a red light, some a blue one, while others simply dim or shade the ordinary white light. Again, it is an individual matter; choose that which seems best for you. The light must be low, however, so that surrounding objects are only dimly perceived. Later in your development you can increase the light, but at first it is best that you should have as little distraction as possible from chance reflections in the mirror or crystal.

The crystal or other speculum as these things are sometimes called, should be so placed that the surface can be gazed upon without any strain. Eye strain should particularly be avoided, since this might well produce some adverse effects. The crystal is usually supplied with a small black stand, but if you wish you can simply cradle it in the folds of a piece of black velvet. It is best to place it on a small table so situated that, as we have said, you

can gaze quietly and without strain at its surface.
You can, if you wish, hold the crystal, with its velvet
cushion in the joined palms of your hands, but this
may cause you to worry subconsciously about the
possibility of dropping it, and this worry will not
help you in your development.

Physical and Mental Relaxation

All these conditions are external to you; how
about your internal conditions? The chief mental
condition should be one of quiet intention to sit for
the development of clairvoyant power. The
emotions should be as little disturbed as possible,
and the physical body must be thoroughly relaxed.
This last condition is far too often overlooked, but it
is one of the essential prerequisites for development.

There are various methods of bringing about this
relaxed physical condition, but the exercise we are
now about to give you is, in our estimation, one of
the best.

Sitting with the spine straight, breathe in deeply
through the nose. To do this, start from the
diaphragm (the great muscle which separates the
heart and lungs from the rest of the internal organs)
and then expand the rib-cage until a really full
breath has been taken. The shallow chest, or rather
upper-chest, breathing doesn't really do what is
needed. As you breathe in, transfer your attention
to the top of your head. Now slowly breathe out,
and as you do so, mentally relax first the muscles of
the scalp, then the face muscles, and then in turn
the arms, trunk and legs, right down to the toes.
Repeat this a set number of times. We would
suggest that you take six such deep breaths. You
will find that at first you will tend to tense up again

automatically as soon as your attention has passed from one point to the next, but soon the subconsciousness will obey your will and produce the required relaxation.

You are now ready to take your first step in the development of clairvoyance.

CHAPTER FOUR

VISION

Having dealt as fully as possible in a book of this size with the general theory and conditions of clairvoyant development, we now come to the actual practice of scrying in the crystal or mirror. We will assume that you have carried out the instructions we have given you, and are now sitting in a thoroughly relaxed state of mind and body, gazing quietly and without strain at the surface of the speculum, which may be any one of those we have described. For our present purpose, let us suppose that it is the black mirror which is being used.

'Tickling of the Ant'
At first all that appears to happen is that the surface of the mirror gradually moves out of focus, and you cannot see it very well. Then, quite suddenly, it comes back into sharp detail. This may happen during part or even through the whole of the sitting at your first few attempts. Perhaps you may also become aware of certain bodily sensations. These usually take the form of what

appears to be a tight band round the forehead, and a curious itching or tickling sensation between the eyes, at the root of the nose. This tickling is referred to in some Eastern books as 'the tickling of the ant', and this seems a very good name for it. It *does* feel very much as though some little insect was crawling around under the skin in a circular route of its own. These two happenings, the shifting focus of the eyes and the tight band with the tickling sensation, both seem to be due to purely physical causes, at least at the start of training. The disappearance and reappearance of the mirror is due to the muscles which control the focusing of the lens of the eye becoming tired. As they relax, so the object at which you have been looking drops out of focus. Then, after a while, they tighten up and refocus on the object before them. The tight band and the tickling are due to slight changes in the circulation of the blood in the forehead, though the 'tickling of the ant' indicates that a little-known aspect of the pituitary gland is being brought into activity. Do not be discouraged if this is all your experience in your first few sittings. Rome wasn't built in a day, and these psychic impressions have to cut their new channel between the subconscious and the waking mind.

Further Signs

If you persevere, then other signs will appear. One of the most usual is that the surface seems to gradually cloud over, until it is as though you are looking at a curtain of grey mist which covers its whole extent. Then this curtain of mist may begin to break up and to whirl round in smaller clouds, and brilliant sparks of light flash out all over the mirror. At this stage you are likely to throw back your development by becoming excited over the fact that you are seeing something. This excitement can very effectually destroy the quiet poise of your mind, and so interfere with the tenuous lines of connection which are being built below in the depths of the subconscious.

However, if you can keep your mind in the quiet state, then the appearances in the mirror may begin to increase and to take other forms. Fragmentary glimpses of brilliantly coloured landscapes, faces grave and gay, and luminous coloured clouds may all show themselves, but you will find that it is difficult, at first, to hold any one picture for more than a second or so.

When these landscapes, faces and colours appear, it is evidence that certain psychological changes are taking place in your mind, and it is these changes which will enable the inner vision to be brought to your waking self. These pictures are the first cousins to those curious little pictures which are seen by some people during the entry into sleep and again when awakening from sleep. The psychologists call them hypnogogic images, and assume that they are made and projected by the subconscious. This is true enough, but in our present case, they may be more than just images; they may be message-carrying images, bringing information which has been received by the inner sense. They are, as it were, waking dreams, and have their own definite meaning.

Passive Vision
When you have reached this stage, you have begun to develop clairvoyance. You will discover for

yourself the curious trick of holding the mind in a poised and yet relaxed condition; something which seems impossible at first. Many times you will become suddenly excited at what you see, and the whole vision will close down immediately. You will also find that your visions begin to divide into two distinct groups. One will be much larger than the other, and this may possibly indicate what type of vision you are developing. One set of images will be of normal everyday things, and the other will present symbolic forms to you. You will also find that the symbolic vision seems to be associated with a positive questioning attitude of your mind. The literal vision appears to be reflected into your mind without any effort on your part; it is a passive vision.

Some will tell you that the passive vision is to be avoided, but this is usually suspect and recalls the advice given by the fox which had lost its tail. You will remember he stressed the advantages of having no tail, and suggested to the others that they had *their* tails removed! Whether you discern passively or actively, your gift can be of help to you and to others.

Having succeeded in seeing in the mirror, don't be in too much of a hurry to give a meaning to everything you see therein. A Catholic writer, the late Monsignor Robert Hugh Benson, referring to these visions, said that it was as though you were in a room with a window looking down on a busy street. The window blind is down, so that you cannot see out at all. Then quite suddenly, the blind is pulled aside for a second, and you are looking down at the crowded street. Perhaps, in that momentary glimpse, you see a girl in a red

dress carrying a basket of flowers. Then the blind
cuts off your vision again. You would be very foolish
if you began to argue that the girl was in any way
concerned with you; she simply happened to be
passing when you looked out. So it is with a great
deal of this kind of vision. We have spent many
hours, during sleepless nights, in watching these
vivid pictures in the astral light, without any reason
to think that they were in any way connected with
us personally. There are certain psychic currents
which flow daily around this planet; the Hindus
call them the *Tatvas*, and in each of the five types of
tatvic current one kind of image appears to
predominate. However, that will not directly
concern you at the beginning of your development.

There *are* images, however, which are directly
connected with you. They are images which are
being used by your subconscious mind as a code by
means of which certain information can be passed
through to you. This information may relate to your
own personal inner life and conditions, it may be
definite information regarding others, information
which your inner senses have received, or, in some
cases, it may be due to the action of other minds
which are passing a message through your inner self
into your waking self in this way.

Symbolic Images

Now as you proceed with your development, you
will find that certain images have a symbolic value,
and are the code which your inner self is using. You
will have to learn from your visions what such
symbolic forms *mean to you*. We have stressed these
three words, for they are very important. What a
symbol means to the inner self of one person is not

necessarily the meaning it has for another. To us, the symbol of a cat seen in a vision has to do with Egyptian things, but a friend of ours, who was a very fine clairvoyant found that whenever he saw a similar symbol, it foreshadowed his being ill within a couple of days. He was engaged in lecturing work all over the country, and he told me that this recurring vision often enabled him to write cancelling a lecture engagement in time for those concerned to engage a substitute lecturer!

Here we come to something very important. These symbols, if you see them in a vision, will be found to be of two different kinds. One is seen in a vision without any emotional atmosphere, and you have no clue as to what it might mean. The second type is not only seen, but brings with it definite knowledge as to its meaning. This knowledge which comes immediately with the vision is, in our experience, almost invariably correct. If you see a symbol, and have to stop to interpret what it might mean, then be wary, for your interpretation might possibly be far from the real meaning. Incidentally, when you commence to get a succession of such symbols which you have to interpret for yourself, it is usually a sign that for one reason or another your clairvoyant powers are not working correctly, and you should give them a rest for a time.

There is another point with which we must deal, as we are considering the question of symbols. It applies mostly to those symbols which are interpreted as foreshadowing the future. Many hundreds of times we have heard clairvoyants saying something like this, 'I see a lovely bunch of daffodils above you and this tells me that when the flowers are blooming in the Spring, you will have good news', and so forth. Apart from the fact that flowers bloom long before the Spring, and that Spring covers quite a few weeks, the whole thing is so indefinite that as a supposed clairvoyant impression of the future, it is pretty futile. *If* the prediction cannot be narrowed down to less than a three month period, then as a prediction it doesn't rate very highly. In any case, such vague descriptions strongly suggest that the clairvoyant ability of the person is very poor.

We suggest, therefore, that you train yourself to understand the symbols your inner senses present to you, and also that you endeavour to give clear and definite descriptions, rather than vague generalities. This can be done, but it does mean hard work. However, the results do justify the labour.

Controlling Your Visions

Now when you have gained the power to see the visions you have accomplished half your task. The next highly important thing you must do is to gain the power to shut off your visions. There are far too many 'half-baked' clairvoyants wandering around; people who have begun to open up their psychic sight and then, for one reason or another have never mastered it. They have become involuntary seers, at the mercy of every psychic breeze that blows, and responsive in an automatic negative manner to all kinds of thought currents from those around them. Because of this, their clairvoyant ability, which could have been a great asset to them becomes instead a liability. This can become a really dangerous matter; it is apparent that if one is crossing a busy street, one does not want a sudden vision of the Elysian Fields to appear before one. It might lead to an early residence in the superphysical world.

Closing Down the Psychic Faculties

We advise you, therefore, to train yourself to keep the two levels of consciousness apart after you have had your sitting. Close down the clairvoyance by a calm effort of will. Now this does not mean that you need to grit your teeth and thrust out your jaw or go red in the face in a violent physical effort. To do this is a waste of energy, and is something akin to switching off the electric light by knocking up the switch with a sledge hammer. It may possibly put out the light, but it will almost certainly damage the switch. All you need to do is to quietly tell yourself that you are now finishing the sitting, and closing down the psychic faculty. Then immediately do some normal physical world activity, such as entering up your record of what has happened during the session. If at any time afterwards the clairvoyant sense begins to show itself against your wishes, then *at once* turn your attention away from it. This must be done immediately or you will find that, as the vision forms before you, it will become increasingly difficult to shut it down. You may perhaps feel that if there is a possibility of something harmful happening to you, it would be helpful if a clairvoyant vision could suddenly warn you of impending trouble. This is so, and it can be so arranged that, by a definite mental suggestion which you give yourself, the clairvoyant power will begin to work when anything is likely to happen which may be to your detriment. We owe our life on two occasions at least to such sudden warnings projected into the waking consciousness, but these involuntary activities of the psychic senses are not to be encouraged unless, as we have said, some definite mental suggestion has built up the channel through which they can emerge into consciousness.

We have already suggested to you that it is advisable for you to keep silent about your development until you have both unfolded the power *and* learned to control it. Even then, you will find that if it is known that you have clairvoyant ability, you will be pestered by foolish people who simply desire to see some new thing, or who hope to gain something for themselves. Many of these people, who could well afford to pay for the services of a professional psychic, will see in your gift a splendid chance of getting something for nothing!

Professional Psychism

This brings us to the thorny question of professional psychism. Is it allowable to use this faculty for the purpose of earning a living? As the clairvoyant faculty is an entirely natural power, and not in itself sacrosanct, there is no logical reason why it may not be so employed. However, there are other considerations which must be taken into account. The clairvoyant is to a great extent an artist rather than a technician. His powers are variable, depending upon his inner personal conditions, as well as upon outside factors. Until he has fully stabilized his power, he is not in a position to act as a professional psychic consultant, for he can never tell when the faculty will be available. Later he may be able to take upon himself this very demanding and responsible role, and by maintaining a high ethical standard, can be of great assistance to many people.

Finally, we may say that during some fifty years we have exercised the clairvoyant faculty, without making any charge for our work, and have found a real and lasting satisfaction in the hope we have been able to give to many people. We did, for some three weeks, break our rule and accept payment, but that time was sufficient for us to realise something of the temptations and difficulties which the professional psychic, if he be genuine, has to encounter.

CHAPTER FIVE

SOME FURTHER CONSIDERATIONS

In this chapter I want to give you some practical advice which may help you to avoid some of the pitfalls in the development of the clairvoyant faculty. Of course, the ability to see clearly in the crystal or mirror is the first and a very important part of your training, but it *is* only a part. There is so much which begins to affect you immediately you start work on your development. Some of the sudden changes in both yourself and your general surroundings may seem to be only minor obstacles, but they may possibly escalate into a really annoying difficulty. It is with the object of helping you to avoid some at least of these difficulties that this chapter has been written.

First of all, let us deal with the effect of clairvoyant development upon yourself, and first of all I will deal with the effects which you, personally, experience, and then go on to deal with the effects produced by you upon other people. You must remember that you will become more sensitive, not only on the psychic level, but also in your ordinary life. This abnormal bodily sensitivity should be only a passing phase and should cease when you have more or less completed your training. Unfortunately, there are many psychics who never get out of this stage of undue physical sensitivity, and it is these people who help to give the subject a bad name. This sensitivity usually shows itself in an unusual irritability, usually shortly before you commence a session of endeavouring to see in the crystal or mirror. Every sound seems unduly loud, and you find yourself being impatient and querulous with those around you. In many cases this state also remains with you *after* your session, and can cause a good deal of trouble. It is because of this that the general public has the idea that *all* phychics are pallid, nervous and excitable people, prone to sudden enthusiasms or deep depression. It is these extreme reactions you must learn to control, and thus show to the world that a psychic can be a normal, well-balanced person.

At the commencement of your training, however, it is difficult to avoid these expressions of nervousness and temperamental lack of balance, because they are due, in a greater or lesser degree, to the changes brought about in you by the training you are now undergoing. A similar state of affairs is to be seen when someone begins the rigid training of an athlete in some exacting physical sport. This passes as his body begins to respond to the training, and in the same way temperamental unbalance and acute nervousness will gradually diminish as you proceed with your training. I have said that they are due to the changes wrought in you by that training. What do I mean by that statement? Well, it is very important to remember that contact with the psychic levels allows strong and active forces to be immediately released, and these forces will affect your whole personality. Because your personality is not as yet balanced and integrated, these forces will meet with a certain amount of resistance, and this will result in the unwelcome physical symptoms you may experience. Please don't mistake me here. If I tell you that your personality is not yet balanced, that is something which any psychologist will tell you is true of some 90 per cent of the whole human race! In fact, some psychologists are of the opinion that the truly integrated and balanced personality does not as yet exist upon the earth. This is an extreme view, but nevertheless as a general rule it is true that most of us are, in varying degrees, not properly balanced and integrated as personalities. When the psychic forces are contacted by you as you begin your development, they flow through your personality, arousing various reactions within you, and further upsetting the balance thereof. I am stressing this for I do not want to mislead you. But you will remember I have said that these forces will affect you in greater or *lesser* degree, and I have pointed out that if you correctly work at your training, they will cease to give you trouble.

Cultivation of Humility
One of the most common results of this rush of power when one is in contact with the psychic levels is a feeling of authority – a positive feeling that what

you are getting from those levels is absolutely true and must not be questioned, and the credulous attitude of some around you often increases this feeling of superiority. There is a 'Thus saith the Lord' ring to it. However, *no* psychic communication is entirely correct. Always, because it has to come through the personality of the seer, it is coloured, as I have said before, by the mental and emotional states of the personality. But in the beginning, you may well feel that this or that vision *must* be absolutely correct and you will probably find that you are becoming to some extent intolerant of anyone who queries or dares to disagree with it. Now this positive and authoritative feeling does distinguish your psychic faculty from the results of ordinary mental visualization, and to that extent it can be useful. But *always*, all visions, all contacts with the psychic levels, *must* be checked and tested by your reason. Because of this, it is very helpful if, concurrently with your sessions for clairvoyant development, you meditate upon the ethical virtue of *humility*. Not the hypocritical humility of Charles Dickens's Uriah Heep, but true humility, free from undue self-depreciation and a firm endeavour to realize your own true status, together with a willingness to direct your efforts accordingly. The cultivation of this spirit of humility will not always be easy. Between the hypocritical subservience of Uriah Heep and your own feelings of self-assertion, you will have to steer as the old mariners did when they came to Scylla and Charybdis.

There is a saying which epitomizes this: 'For every step in psychic development, take two in your *moral* development.' If this could always be carried out, it would make life much easier for us when we are working in this psychic field, but under the conditions in which we work, this is largely a counsel of perfection as our Catholic friends would say. Nevertheless, it must be carried out to some extent at least, if we wish to develop to the best advantage. If you approach your psychic development in this spirit of true humility, then you will not be swept away by any rush of power from the psychic levels.

At the same time, you must not allow yourself to unduly minimize what you get, by saying 'It's just my imagination'. The psychic faculties work through the subconscious mind, and that part of the mind is exceedingly susceptible to suggestion, so any negative suggestions are accepted as easily as positive ones. The golden rule is, do not try to criticize whatever may appear in the crystal or mirror until *after* the session, when the subconscious sensitivity to suggestion has decreased. Of course, in the beginning, as I have said before, perhaps 95 per cent of what you see *will* be the product of your visual imagination, but as you continue to develop, that percentage will alter, until, when you are fully developed, 95 per cent of what you see will be truth-telling and accurate.

Always, of course, there will remain that small percentage of 'stained glass' due to the psychic impressions having to come through your personality. This can never be entirely eliminated, but you can learn to make allowance for it, in the same way as one fires a little off target if the gun we are using has a bias of some kind such as 'throwing to the right'; one would then fire somewhat to the left of the target in order to correct this. So, if you perceive the 'stained glass' in the visions you receive, you can reduce it to a minimal proportion. Now such distortion is very largely due to the condition of your physical health plus your mental and emotional reactions at the time. You must learn to gain some measure of control of all three, if your clairvoyance is to be accurate.

Yoga

For this reason, apart from other benefits which may accrue to you, I would recommend to you that, in addition to your sessions for clairvoyant development, you should also follow a schedule of regular sessions for relaxation and meditation. It is not necessary to join this or that group, or to work under some Eastern Guru. The theory and practice of meditation have both been fully explained – as far as they will affect you – in a good many books which are available at the present time. There are Yoga classes being run by the authorities in many schools and other centres of education in many of our large towns, and the same pattern is being repeated overseas in many countries. But as I have said, you can obtain all the information you will need from some of the excellent books which have been written on the subject. For your purpose, a simplified form of relaxation technique, and an equally simple method of meditation will be quite sufficient, and as you continue to use these techniques, you will begin to see how very helpful they can be to you in the development of your faculty.

I would like to stress the importance of keeping a detailed record of the results of your sessions for clairvoyant development. This record is best made *immediately* after the session itself, before the mind has had a chance to forget the details of your vision. There is a reason for this. When you are beginning to bring through the clairvoyant vision, it has to compete with the normal physical vision, and this, because of its long-established evolutionary history as the normal way of acquiring knowledge, is far stronger than the first tentative gleams of the newly emerging psychic faculty. For this reason, the finer details of the vision are quickly lost – 'They fly forgotten as a dream' – and indeed they do partake of the nature of dreams, springing, as they do, from below the threshold of consciousness. As you log down your successes, so equally you must set down your failures, for very often failures can be more helpful than successes. They call your attention to some persistent condition which you may have entirely overlooked.

Record the Truth
Since the state of your physical health, together with your mental and emotional conditions at the time of your session are all three of importance, they should be noted down each time, and since our general mental and emotional outlook is often moulded, to some extent, by the weather, this should also be recorded. Over a period of say three months, you will probably find that there is some definite correlation between the high success points, and the lunar positions should also be included, for there is good evidence to show that the moon does have some effect upon our mental and emotional states. Such a record, covering the various influences which may affect you will help you to develop your faculty and use it with discretion and

discrimination. For instance, visions seen during the dark of the moon should be carefully scrutinized for traces of distortion, since it is the common experience of very many seers that it is at this period that such distortion is likely to take place.

But, and this is a big but, you must be absolutely honest with yourself – the record must be like Caesar's wife, above suspicion, even though it may be mentally and emotionally painful for you to record it. From personal experience, I know how difficult it can be to acknowledge, even in a private record, that you have not succeeded. We none of us like to admit failure, so when we are experiencing a series of negative results, we tend to try to make the record look better than it really is, and our imagination can get to work. 'I'm sure I did see some flashes of light in the mirror', or 'I'm sure there *was* a shadowy picture forming, and it might have become clearer if I'd gone on with the sitting'. If the faculty starts developing, you will not need to say such things, for even the first tentative flashes of the clairvoyant power will make a positive impression on you. Whilst we are dealing with this part of the training, may I strongly advise you to sit each time for a certain period, say half an hour. No matter what is happening at the end of that time, you must stop. Your subconscious must be trained to obey the orders you give. You must always be in control of things.

By keeping a true record, and checking your visions against the varying factors of health, lunar position and emotional-mental states of mind during the session, it may often happen that you will begin to see a pattern emerging. Thus it may be that you are more successful in scrying in the mirror or crystal when the moon is at the full, or you may discover that if you are in contact with certain people just before you commence your session, such contact will appear to affect your work during the session. At a later stage in your development, the influence of such people can be cut off, so that it ceases to affect you, but in the beginning of training you will have to cope with it. The golden rule is to keep a detailed record. This record must be a truthful and *regular* record of all your sessions. It is good self-discipline, and also provides you with an *external objective check* upon your subjective psychic experiences. In most of us, too, it can be very useful in preventing us getting swollen heads or inflated egos! At the beginning of your training you should take advantage of every favourable condition, but as you advance you should try to scry under more difficult conditions. If you can then obtain good results, you will have made yourself still more independent of outside influences, and this will strengthen your whole personality. In any case it will help you to bring your faculty to a higher level. Always remember that you must never cease your efforts to perfect your psychic vision. There are unlimited depths within you still to be explored, and your psychic vision must be continually enlarging its field of operation. There is no finality in this field of research.

Group Clairvoyance

I have referred to the influence which certain people may seem to have. This is a very real thing, and such people can help your faculty to grow or very definitely inhibit it. If you are sitting in a group for psychic development, the combined psychic and

mental forces of those forming the group will
continually be working subconsciously to bring
your clairvoyant faculty up to a certain level. This is
determined by the general mental level of the
group, and once it is reached, the group influence
will tend to fix it at this level. Now, although the
psychic forces of the other members of the group
can be such a limiting or a stimulating factor it is
mainly a hindering one, tending to make your
vision agree with the general outlook of the group.
Not only can you be conditioned by the group-
mind, but, as I have said elsewhere in this book, you
can begin to unconsciously rely upon the stimulus
of the group-mind, until you may become unduly
dependent upon it and can do no good psychic work
if you are not able to work with the other members
of the group. This is a very real danger, and must be
taken into account. On the other hand, of course,
the level of the group-mind may be much higher
than your own, in which case there is a helpful
tuning up of your faculty to a higher level of
perception.

It often happens, in such groups that there occur
regular periods of psychic tension, when the
individual members are themselves being tuned in
to higher levels of consciousness, and as this
happens, you, or any other developing psychic in
that group has the opportunity to expand the scope
of his psychic abilities.

Some groups, however, seem to provide a *fixed*
mental atmosphere in which the psychic faculties of
all the members are stuck at one level. That great
occultist, Dion Fortune, in the course of her
teaching, insisted that we should recognize this
limiting factor in the group mind and make

allowance for it. Sometimes it would seem that the best thing to do is to leave the group entirely, and this you must be prepared to do if you find that the atmosphere of the group is beginning to hinder your progress.

But before you take this step, it is as well if you devote some time to seriously considering whether it is the whole group or simply you yourself that is out of step. When one has begun to get some results, it is very easy to resent any criticism believing it to be due to the jealousy of those who have as yet got no results. Again, the virtue of true humility is indicated. Because all in the group are for the time being in a sensitive condition, it is very easy for trouble to arise, so carefully make sure that you are acting correctly before you take the extreme step of leaving the group.

Psychic Catalysts

Now for a rather interesting aspect of the subject. There are people who, if they become members of a psychic group, have a strange effect on the workings of that group. *Their very presence* appears to either stimulate or inhibit any psychic happenings. In most cases they do not appear to develop any psychic faculty themselves, but they do definitely affect others as I have said. In chemistry, certain substances have been found to do the same thing in chemical reactions. They appear to start all kinds of chemical reactions in whatever mixtures they are placed, but they do not enter into chemical combination with any other substance in the mixture. They are known generally as catalysts. The people I am speaking of may be regarded as psychic catalysts, and seem to have certain physical characteristics – for instance they are very often auburn haired. We do not, as yet have much detailed knowledge as to why these people affect psychic development, and they are not numerous. But if you should join a group which has one such person as a member, then you will quickly find that the group is very successful in developing the psychic faculties of its members, or else it is entirely unsuccessful and on its way out.

You will see that there are both opportunities and limitations affecting you if you join a group for psychic development, and it is for you to choose for yourself whether you will join such a group or go it alone in your training. The advice and expertise of the leaders of the group, together with the encouragement of working with others is a positive factor, but how expert those leaders may be, and the general make-up of the group, may well make you prefer to work on your own. Personally, I would advise you to work on your own, as I have said earlier in this book. Of course one other person who could record the happenings during the sessions would be helpful. Working in this way you are not so liable to become dependent upon others. However, it is for you to decide.

Immediate Knowledge
Now I want to come to another important aspect of your training. Apparently, it is not connected with your scrying in the mirror or crystal, but actually it is very closely connected with it. As you sit gazing into the mirror, there may come certain mental impressions, even though you have not yet obtained objective vision. Such impressions are of two kinds. One class is made up of those results of

the working of your clairvoyant faculty which are being directed to your efforts at seeing in the mirror, but which, for one reason or another, cannot be made objective. As your training proceeds, these impressions decrease, because they are now working directly with your increasing power to project them in objective form in the mirror. The second class is entirely different, and is in itself a distinct form of clairvoyance. Here the impressions are clear and defined, and they arise in your mind as you are scrying in the mirror, or they may appear spontaneously afterwards. These impressions are neither objective nor subjective *images*, but are a kind of *immediate knowledge* which appears in your consciousness. Although you see no form whatsoever, yet you become aware that something of a certain size and shape is before you, and you find that you can describe it in detail. It 'as if' you saw it, but you don't see it! Very confusing, this explanation; but when you experience this 'formless seeing' you will realize what I am trying to tell you. This form of clairvoyance has been termed 'seeing a black cat at midnight at the bottom of a coal mine'. Although you *see* nothing at all a detailed idea arises in your mind of a definite person or thing, and the details are absolutely clean-cut, there is nothing vague about them, once this strange form of awareness has commenced to develop.

At first it is terribly difficult for one to rely on these impressions, for we are conditioned by ages of evolution to associate sight with the physical eyes. Here we are not using our physical eyes to pick up the impressions, though we may be looking into the mirror awaiting vision. I believe that what is happening is that we are beginning to use the true psychic senses which are independent of the physical senses, and are thus supplementing our mirror vision by this extra information. When you are fairly well advanced in your training you will find that these flashes of intuitive knowledge are beginning to form a continuous background to your mirror visions. You not only see your mentally projected vision in the mirror, you also receive a detailed packet of information which enters your mind at the same time. There is an ancient form of psychism which depends upon the involuntary nervous system which also shows itself in vague impressions, but without the clarity and detail of the intuitive clairvoyance. This atavistic psychic ability seems to be possessed by a good many animals and certain human beings whose intellectual level is not very high – though they may be very intelligent and well able to deal with life. But the intuitive clairvoyance cannot work through them because it comes from a higher mental level than any that they can work upon. But there *is* a form of impressional clairvoyance which they can develop; as I have pointed out, it lacks the clearness and detail of the intuitive type.

Intuitive Clairvoyance

But to return to the intuitive clairvoyance. It arises in a higher aspect of the mind than the other ancient form, and is therefore far more reliable.

I have referred to it as intuitional psychism so perhaps I should make a few remarks about intuition. There is much talk about this. It is sneered at as being a feminine possession, used by the ladies to assert their own peculiar point of view

in the teeth of the reasonable statements made by
'rational' people – usually male! When as so often
happens, the lady's intuition proves to be correct, it
is usually dismissed as sheer coincidence. However,
intuition is a common possession, and is not
confined to the female sex, but is to be found in all
mankind in varying degree. The dependence of man
upon his reasoning ability has caused his intuitive
powers to weaken, and they are unable, except
under exceptional circumstances, to rise into his
consciousness. Any attempt at systematic
development of the psychic faculties, and any
serious effort to master the art of meditation will
tend to arouse the intuitive power. As I have said,
this intuitive power comes from a high level in the
mind and is not a matter of general impressions,
but is detailed and accurate. More to the point,
intuitional psychism is linked up with the *ethical* and
moral content of our lives, and is therefore an aid to
ethical and moral judgments.

Let us take one instance of this. We will suppose
that we have two clairvoyants. One has developed
objective vision in the mirror or crystal, the other
has developed the intuition type of subjective
perception. The objective clairvoyant sees in the
mirror the appearance of someone, whom, judging
from his face and general appearance, would seem
to be a respectable and honest person, and even of
outstanding character. Our objective clairvoyant is
inclined to take this vision at its face value, but the
intuitive clairvoyant, although he sees no objective
form, draws quite different conclusions, and
perceives that the person seen has a basic character
which differs greatly from his normal image – he is
not so respectable nor is he so benevolent as the

objective clairvoyant judged him to be. Physical contact with the person who has been seen clairvoyantly will prove that the intuitive seer was correct. It seems, therefore, that a combination of the two forms of seership is a goal to be aimed at. You will then not only see appearances in the mirror, but you will immediately understand the meaning of what you see. It is because I believe this to be the correct method of development that I have suggested that you sit for meditation for a fixed time each day, as this will open up the intuitive powers.

Symbols

There are many books on meditation, and many groups engaged in its practice, but I would suggest that you employ the particular system which I suggest to you later on in this chapter. As we have noted earlier on, much of your clairvoyance may come through in the shape of symbols. It has been said, somewhat unkindly, that symbols are the refuge of the inefficient clairvoyant – if he can't get definite pictures, he can always fall back upon symbols! This may well be so in quite a large number of cases, but nevertheless symbols play a large part in psychic vision. Indeed, when we come to the consideration of the deeper spiritual verities, we are forced to fall back on symbolism. A classical case is that book in the New Testament known as The Revelation of St John. Here the bulk of the book is purely symbolic. In connection with this book, it is interesting to note that when the seer would have fallen at the feet of the Being who was his guide and instructor in the vision, the Angel forbade him, saying 'See thou do it not, for I also am thy *fellow-servant*.'

Now the symbols which arise in your mind are of several kinds. First, there are those symbols which arise in dreams. These are mainly concerned with your internal mental states, but occasionally they are psychic coming up 'through the Gates of Horn' as the ancients used to put it. The study and manipulation of the dream symbols is the greater part of the craft of the psychologist and psychiatrist. But there are other symbols which have grown up in an haphazard fashion within your mind, and when your clairvoyance begins to develop it will tend to use those symbols. However, it is possible for you to build up a planned and selected code of symbols and to persuade your psychic faculties to use it. Should you attempt this, you must be prepared for a certain amount of resistance from your own subconsciousness, which usually strongly prefers its own home-made code! But just as the work of a skilled craftsman is usually superior to the efforts of the do-it-yourself amateur, so the system which I am very briefly going to describe has many points of advantage over the home-made code of the average subconscious mind. Before I go any further, I must assure you that what I shall give you is only a very small part of a very great philosophy known as the Qabalah. The organized symbol-system we shall touch upon is the master-symbol of the Qabalah. Within the limits of this small book it is impossible for me to give you more than a fraction of the philosophy of the Qabalah, but books on the subject by Dion Fortune, Dr Israel Regardie, myself and many other writers are available.

Qabalistic Symbolism

Without going into more than a general

explanation of the Qabalistic system as far as it concerns your psychic training, I may say that the basis of this philosophy is that Man is the Microcosmic reflection of the Macrocosm or Universe in which he lives, and by this theory, all the powers and forces of that Universe are to be found in him. Upon this basis a wonderful scheme of philosophy has been built up by the Qabalists, but we are only concerned here with that part which has relevance to our efforts at psychic development.

The accompanying diagram gives you the main idea of the Tree of Life as it is called. Each of the key points or Sephiroth, as they are called (singular is 'Sephirah'), has certain names, symbols and ideas connected with it. These represent certain factors in the universe and also in Man. For the present we are only concerned with what they mean as far as our clairvoyant training is concerned. You will notice that the qualities shown on the Sephiroth are complementary, balancing each other, and in this philosophy any permanent unbalance of the forces is undesirable. So vertically KETHER balances MALKUTH, the Kingdom as it is called; horizontally, the two outer 'Pillars' are in complementary opposition with each other, CHOKMAH balancing BINAH; GEBURAH doing the same with GEDULAH, and NETZACH and HOD complementing each other at the bases of the two outer Pillars. Incidentally, these two Pillars are sometimes given the names of the two Pillars in front of King Solomon's Temple, which were known as Jachin and Boaz. On the central Pillar, the sephirah TIPHARETH is the symbol and Station of Balance, whilst below it YESOD represents Foundations. MALKUTH, the Kingdom of Matter, being the state where alone all the values of the Tree are finally worked out and determined. Unless a principle is worked out in Malkuth, it is incomplete.

Now in order to use this symbol in your development, it will be necessary for you to meditate upon each symbol in turn, trying to realize and understand its particular meaning, until the symbol with its meanings is firmly established in your subconscious mind. You will realize, of course, that you will have to persevere steadily at these meditations repeating the same subjects again and again, until you have made a permanent impression upon your subconscious. You will notice that each Sephirah is given a definite colour, and there is also a definite idea attached to it.

Significance of Colour

Geburah is fiery red, and the idea of breaking down and destroying is linked with it. Gedulah, on the other hand, is blue and the idea of construction is given to it. Netzach is emerald green, and the idea is of emotional feeling, whilst Hod is coloured orange which is linked with the idea of intellect. Yesod is violet and its idea is that of foundation, and Malkuth is given four colours, one for each quarter, olive, citrine, russet and black respectively. Its idea is 'Kingdom', where all other things come to fruition. Tiphareth is coloured gold, and carries the idea of Balance and Harmony. Binah is indigo blue, and carries the idea of restriction, inertia and the retention of established things. Chokmah is silver, with the associated idea of unlimited force at tremendous pressure, and finally, Kether is pure

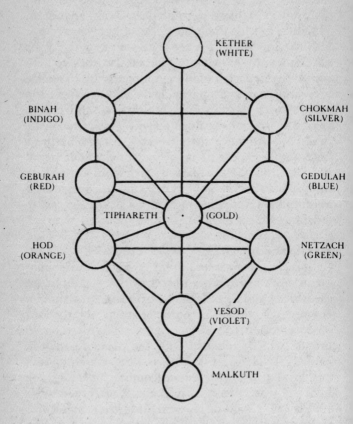

THE TREE OF LIFE

white and the idea it carries is that of the One Source from which all else proceeds, the primal energy source of the Universe and of Man.

To do your meditations, you should now make ten square pieces of white card and colour them with the colours I have given you here. You should leave a strip at the bottom of the card unpainted, and a similar strip at the top. In the top space write or print the name of the card, Hod or Binah or whatever it may be, and in the bottom strip the idea associated with it. Now you have a pack of coloured cards, one of which must be used each day as the focus point of your meditation. In that meditation you should very carefully consider the idea connected with the card chosen for the day, trying to realize exactly what it implies. During the rest of the day, you should look around you and try to see where the idea is being worked out in life. Let me give you an example. You have been meditating on Geburah this morning (the best time for this kind of meditation *is* early in the morning, and I shall assume that you have done your meditation shortly after arising and before going to work). Now, as you go down the street, and also when you are at work, you will be on the alert for any instance around you of the principle of breaking-down and destroying. Perhaps, as you went down the street and saw the bull-dozers demolishing a house. This is a perfect symbol of destruction. Then, when at work you may see that a part of some department is being closed down and no longer used. Again the element of destruction is there.

I have chosen this particular Station on the Tree because it makes it easy for me to illustrate another point. Destruction can be of two kinds. One is to

simply clear the ground in readiness for new
activities. The old slum is bull-dozed in order that
on the cleared ground new and better houses can be
built. You can multiply such incidents, where the
destruction is justified because of the improvement
it brings. But it may be that a house in your road
has become empty and derelict, and the vandals
have moved in, breaking windows and smashing in
doors, stripping everything they can find, and
reducing the place to a dirty and noisome shell. *This*
form of destruction is out of balance, since it serves
no good purpose, and there is no constructive idea
behind it. You picture in your mind your square of
brilliant red and change that colour to one of dirty
red, and the idea of wanton destruction. In the
course of the day you will be observing other
examples of the working out of this principle of
Geburah. The following day you will meditate upon
the blue Card of Gedulah, and will be on the look-
out for any examples of constructive work around
you. Equally, if you see an instance of over-
construction and obstructive conservatism, you will
associate it in your mind with a dirty-blue card.
And so with the rest of the Sephiroth. The pure
colour represents the balanced working of the
principle, the dirty colour represents that same
principle out of balance, and therefore relatively
evil.

Colours and Concepts
You are building up a mental filing system with
ten compartments, and associating each
compartment with a colour and a concept. There
was a Russian scientist, Pavlov by name, who did
something similar with dogs, so that when he rang a

bell they immediately showed all the signs of violent hunger and dribbled at the mouth. The process was known as the 'conditioned reflex' and one school of psychology regards this as one of the key points in its behaviourist philosophy. You are establishing a similar series of conditioned reflexes in your mind, so that by the natural association of ideas, every time you come across the working out of the concepts which have been printed on the cards you are using, the mental image of the card immediately comes up in your mind. These associated images can be used by your clairvoyant faculty to pass information through to your waking consciousness. Let me give you another example. You see in your mirror the appearance of someone who, as far as you can judge, is a perfectly ordinary citizen, and one who seems to be of good character, if his clothes and general appearance are anything to go by. Now *if you have done your meditation as you should have done*, there may suddenly flash out above his head the red square which is associated in your mind with the idea of 'breaking-down'. Now this is your *intuitive* clairvoyance giving you its inner perception of his *character*. So the symbol-system is an excellent means by which your intuitive vision can be developed and trained. Each colour symbol should be meditated on in turn, taking them in pairs where they are shown opposite each other on the diagram. Thus Chokmah one day, Binah the next; Hod one day and Netzach the next, and so on.

Incidentally, though you may see the symbol appear above the head of the appearance in the mirror, it can also happen that the colour itself will suffuse and tint the whole clairvoyant picture in the mirror, like a mist, varying in its density according to the amount of the particular quality which is perceived with the appearance. With practice, as the symbols rise in the clairvoyant consciousness, your mind begins to work with them in the same way that it would if you were learning the Morse Code, for instance. At first, as you hear the three dots of the morse for the letter 'S', you consciously count the number of the dots, but as you gain proficiency, the number is entirely forgotten, and your mind simply records the idea of the letter 'S'.

At a later stage you subconsciously interpret the code signals, and the actual words and sentences automatically appear in your consciousness as you listen to the clatter of the Morse instrument. So with the use of the Qabalistic symbols. With increasing expertise, you come to the point where the symbols, deeply imbedded in your subconscious mind by constant meditation upon them, never need to appear in pictorial form, but the information they bring through will surface in your mind in the same way as the words and sentences do in the Morse reception I have used as an example.

Of course, there is much more to learn, but this method, as I have briefly described it, will carry you quite a distance in your development and will make your clairvoyance far more reliable. Remember, objective clairvoyance, whether you see it in the mirror or apparently in space around you, gives you what one may describe as the 'form' of whatever you see, but the intuitive vision shows you the *character* of what it is you are seeing.

Evolving Your Own System
Of course, it is not necessary for you to undertake

the Qabalistic system I have outlined. I have a
natural preference for it, as it is the system upon
which I myself was trained. Very possibly, your
own inner self may work out its own home-made
symbolism system which may be quite effective for
you. So don't be scared, and feel that the whole
thing has become far too intricate for you. The
method I have outlined is a standard one in many of
the groups working along these lines, and has
proved its efficacy. But in this subject there are
shallows where much good work can be done
without special training of this type, as well as deep
waters where only the expertly trained and tested
seers may dare to swim. It may well be that,
working in the shallow waters, you may be able to
give better service to your fellow man than if you
tried to work in the great depths. There is a Hindu
concept known as Adikara. It means 'competence',
and is a reminder that we do best in that work *for
which we are naturally fitted.*

At the same time we should always remember
that we are not rigidly slotted into one level of life –
we can move into the deeper waters if and when we
are prepared for them. In connection with this idea,
I would point out that in the Catechism of the
Church of England, the child is made to say ' ...
and to do my duty in that stage of life *unto which it
shall please God to call me*'.

As you continue to use your clairvoyant faculty in
the service of God and your fellows, it may well
happen that your inner spiritual self may impel and
guide you into the deeper levels of clairvoyant
perception, and the range of your powers may be
deepened and extended. Other psychic faculties
may develop spontaneously. Clairaudience, for

example, and this may progress in the same way as your clairvoyance, becoming in its further stages the formless apprehension of knowledge which is sometimes known as 'The Voice of the Silence', and which is the method of communication between your inner spiritual self and your outer personality. Or other faculties may begin to show themselves, for it very often happens that the habitual use of one faculty will arouse others, as I have said.

In conclusion I would expand a little upon a remark I made earlier in this book. I hinted that quite apart from all the various groups which are developing and using the psychic faculties in conjunction with their own particular systems of philosophies, there are people not to be found in organizations and groups, 'Orders' and 'Fraternities' of the usual kind. They form what may be described as a Withdrawn Order. They never advertise their existence, though in many cases they work through and behind the leaders and members of groups, though they are not to be confused with them, for they never belong to the group-minds of these organizations. Membership of this Withdrawn Order is never canvassed for by them. When you arrive at the point where your spiritual as well as your psychic development warrants it, you may be invited to join their ranks. The choice is entirely yours – there is no compulsion of any kind. Also, whether you elect to carry on in your own quiet way, developing your psychic faculty and using it for the helping of those who need help, or whether you feel drawn to one or other of the many esoteric groups around at the present day, lies entirely within your own choice.

POSTSCRIPT

In this little book we have tried to give a simple and fairly clear outline of clairvoyant development, but we would ask readers to remember that it *is* only an outline. For instance, we have not gone into the symbolism and meaning of the colours which you will perceive clairvoyantly. This omission is because the whole question of colour symbolism is somewhat confused; different authorities giving different interpretations. As we have observed during our own work in this field that the inner mind of each seer tends to put its own meaning upon the colours and symbols which it perceives, it is far better for the reader to learn by a process of trial and error what the symbol code of his or her own inner self is, rather than try to impose the code of some other person upon it.

As you commence your training in clairvoyant perception you will very probably come into contact with others who are interested in the subject or who are themselves attempting such training. In one way this companionship with others who are treading the same path of development as yourself can be most helpful, especially if you are one to whom close human companionship is important. Much depends upon your temperamental make-up. However, such close companionship in the work of psychic training has both advantages and disadvantages and you would do well to consider very carefully whether your association with those who are drawn to you, or you to them, because of your psychic training is really so necessary or helpful.

It may seem to you that we are trying to turn you into a cold-blooded and reserved being, intent only upon your own development. This is not so but, in this matter of psychic training and especially in its earlier stages, there are many who, far from helping you in your endeavours, will almost certainly interfere with them and slow down your development. Not that they proceed by any malice aforethought as a general rule, but by their blundering activities they upset the very delicate conditions under which that development takes place.

In psychic training we find that telepathy is one of the many factors which we have to take into account. The unconscious telepathic action exerted upon you by others is a very real thing and may well hinder your development. For this reason alone it is not wise to allow too many people to know of your attempts at psychic training. Some may be ignorantly contemptuous of your efforts, and this critical contempt will be quickly picked up by your subconscious mind as your sensitivity increases. This will cause an unnecessary strain to be placed on you.

It may well happen also, that you will be invited to join some group of people whose members are also interested in, or actually developing, psychic ability, and here you ought to be very careful indeed. Some of these groups and circles are connected with and work in, the general atmosphere of certain religious sects which have been built up around psychic phenomena. Others are linked with various occult fraternities, good and bad, and others again are based upon the use, or abuse, of the psychedelic drugs. All these groups are usually eager to enlist new recruits, and if such recruits are already working with psychic things, then they are the more eagerly sought after by some of these groups.

Group Membership

There are two other points in connection with development in a group, and they are of the greatest importance to the person who is developing clairvoyance. First of all, membership of a group, though it may afford some measure of protection to the developing psychic during the earlier stages of his work, can very effectively hinder him later on. He may well find that when his clairvoyant ability has become more or less stabilized he has come up against the composite mind of the group, and this group-mind can very definitely limit the scope of his clairvoyance. In a group where the leaders are aware of this and take measures to counteract it, all will be well, but so many groups clearly show that their leaders are 'the blind, leading the blind'. It is better to work on your own, even though you may crave the support and encouragement which a group can give, than to become the prisoner of a group-mind, however high sounding its claims may be.

Secondly, the clairvoyance developed in a group is something of a hot-house plant as a general rule. Though it may work well in the group conditions it will tend to become intermittent and less reliable when used apart from the group. We have often seen this happen. These stricutres do not apply, of course, to a well-run and disciplined group, but such groups are few and hard to find, so that generally speaking we would advise you, as we have already said, to work independently for quite a time until you feel that you can use your new faculty without its being influenced to any degree by the thought-currents of the group.

However, the effect of your clairvoyant development will probably cause you to begin to study the whole subject (of which this clairvoyant faculty is only one aspect), and this will bring you into touch with many of those organizations of which we have spoken. As we have said, such contacts should be avoided in the early stages of your development, but when your faculty has become stabilized and you have gone some way in the development of that virtue of discrimination of which we have spoken, you may begin to study these other aspects of development.

Controlling Your Powers

As soon as you begin to exhibit any clairvoyant power you will be besieged by people who want you to exercise your gift for them. In the first flush of successful development you may well fall into this trap, and exhaust yourself by attempting to gratify the appetite for wonders which is the real reason for these demands upon you. Then you may well find that the faculty begins to be erratic and finally ceases to function. You will then observe with what alacrity and ease those to whose love of sensation you have been ministering will drop you like a red-hot coal and flock after another seer. We have seen it happen on many occasions, which is why we have given you this warning against allowing yourself to be used in such a way.

It is all very well to develop clairvoyance, but the very next step you must take is to gain positive control over the new faculty. Not only must it not function without your conscious permission (except in the very exceptional cases which we have already mentioned), but it should be capable of being used without the need for any special conditions. In effect, you should be able to use it positively whilst you are standing on a busy railway platform, surrounded by noise and bustle. Such adverse conditions should not affect its working.

Further Study

Now, as we have said, you will probably be drawn into the study of the whole subject, and having stabilized your power it will be safe for you to investigate the various groups and societies which are concerned with the subject. You will soon discover that they make up a very mixed bag indeed. Some of them you will find to be of a religio-philosophical nature, whilst others are sectarian religious bodies, Christian and non-Christian in their approach, whilst others are devoted to occult philosophies of many kinds, some of which, as we have already pointed out, are best left alone.

Then there are those which deal with these subjects from the psychological and scientific angle, and the one common factor shared by them all is a hearty damnation of each other!

The literature of the subject you will find to be equally diverse. Some of the periodicals are the house-magazines of the various organizations, others have managed to achieve publication by their own merit, and many more would never have achieved the dignity of a book form if they had been forced to pass the scrutiny of a publisher's reader. This last remark does not mean that *all* that is privately published on these subjects is of no value. Sometimes a book which would have no commercial appeal, and which therefore does not interest average publishers who have to consider the commercial angle, may have considerable merit, and it is desirable, therefore, that it should be published. In this case, private publication is helpful. It might even happen that *your* record of your own clairvoyant development might be of sufficient value for it to be published.

There are many other considerations, but you will find, if you keep a true and faithful record of *all* your sittings and *all* the results you obtain, that you will be able to understand in an increasing degree the wider aspects of your power. Do not forget, the misses as well as the hits must be recorded. Be honest with yourself, and your faculty will give you true information, but if, because of a desire to be thought an infallible oracle, you distort the knowledge you receive in this way, if you make false statements as to what you perceive, then your clairvoyant faculty will deteriorate and become unreliable. Remember, too, what we have already told you: that you assume a very grave responsibility when you use these powers in your dealings with your fellow men. If, however, you commence and continue your clairvoyant career in the spirit which we have already indicated, the desire to know in order to serve, then you will find, as we found many years ago, that you will be led into a path of increasing service and increasing happiness.

More than this: to some of us who have developed the inner vision, glimpses have been gained of a mighty Will in the service of which is to be found true freedom and perfect peace.

So may it be with you who essay this path of practical clairvoyant development.

INDEX